Proceeds from the sale of this book support The War Amps of Canada, 2827 Riverside Drive, Ottawa, Ontario, K1V 0C4. www.waramps.ca

Founded in 1918 to provide returning war amputees with counselling, self-help and practical assistance, The War Amps is a registered charitable organization funded by public support of its Key Tag and Address Label Service. It provides bilingual services to amputees across Canada through its Child Amputee (CHAMP) Program, Adult Amputee Programs, National Amputee Centre and its Service Bureau for war amputees.

355.134 COO C.1
Cooke, Walter, 1936-
Contempt for danger : legends
of Victoria Cross recipients a

Guelph Public Library

MAR X X 2006

CONTEMPT FOR DANGER

LEGENDS OF VICTORIA CROSS RECIPIENTS
AND OTHER CANADIAN MILITARY HEROES

"They placed the lives of others ahead of their own"

WALTER COOKE

©2005 Walter Cooke
All Rights Reserved. No part of this publication may be reproduced,
stored in a retrieval system, or transmitted in any form by any means,
electronic, mechanical, photocopying, recording or otherwise without
written permission from the author.

Except for brief quotations embodied in critical articles or reviews.

Printed in Canada

Copies of Contempt For Danger may be ordered from:
www.contempt4danger.com

355.134
COO

Library and Archives Canada Cataloguing in Publication

Cooke, Walter, 1936-
    Contempt for danger : legends of Victoria Cross recipients and
other Canadian military heroes / Walter Cooke.

Includes index.
ISBN 0-9738346-0-9

    1. Victoria Cross. 2. Heroes--Canada--Biography. 3. Canada-
-Armed Forces--Biography. I. Title.

CR4885.C65 2005   355.1'34'092271   C2005-904491-8

Table of Contents

Older Than Canada	1
Birth of a Nation	8
Sea to Shining Sea	11
Embracing the West	13
Canadian Expeditionary Force	18
Sam Steele	24
The Boer War	27
An Exciting New Century	32
Call to War	35
Ypres, Belgium	38
The Somme, France	44
Ridge of Death	51
Hill 70	56
Passchendaele, Belgium	64
War in the Air	74
Bishop & Barker	80
Spring 1918	85
Amiens, France	89
The Canadian Cavalry Brigade	98
The Hindenburg Line	104
Canal du Nord, France	110
Mons, France	115
Peace	124
Signs of the Times	128
Call to Arms	132

Opening Salvos	138
World Conflagration	143
Dieppe, France	152
Oran, Algeria	159
On the Offensive	163
Objective Maungdaw, Burma	172
Melfa River, Italy	174
Devil's Brigade	177
Juno Beach	181
Air Force Blue	189
Battle for Europe	198
Smokey Smith	205
Camp X	209
Penetrating the Reich	213
Victory in Europe	219
Victory over Japan	224
Epilogue	231

Foreword

Walter Cooke's *Contempt For Danger* is an important and timely book dealing with, as the subtitle says, Legends of Victoria Cross Recipients and other Canadian military heroes.

It is a real privilege to write the Foreword. Sincerely, there is no hesitation on my part in endorsing the book. It is an historical volume whose time has come.

Canadians – and in particular Canadian youth – are anxious to have authoritative reading material dealing with our military heritage. Ex-military personnel who served in combat are quick to accept the awarding of a Victoria Cross as the crowning achievement of those courageous Canadians who are described on the cover of the book as: "They placed the lives of others ahead of their own."

One of the major achievements of the book is that it contains descriptions of the citation of Victoria Cross recipients, which numbered seventy-one from the Great War and sixteen from World War II. Other gallantry decorations are included. In the narratives, the author has prompted us to expand our knowledge of prominent battles. Such are brought to light by incorporating details of military personnel who showed outstanding courage and were recognized by the award of a medal which would, for all time, be a measure of the courage of individual Canadians – and of Canadians as a whole.

Contempt for Danger

The author gives us an opportunity to stretch our minds regarding historical events by including not only the details of specific battles, but what amounts to a 'running commentary' on the events which shaped these wars. It is perhaps trite to say that *Contempt For Danger* is a 'must-read.' The word itself will be perceived as an invitation to learn not only of the strategic side of our military endeavors but, as well, as an excellent history lesson, particularly of the wheres and whyfors of our military combat tasks in the 20th Century.

H. Clifford Chadderton, CC, O.Ont., CLJ, CAE, DCL, LLD

H. Clifford Chadderton is a decorated war hero as well as a staunch champion of humanity.

In June 1944 young Chadderton stormed ashore at Juno Beach in Normandy, France with the Winnipeg Rifles. Over the next four months he remained in the thick of battle as the famed Canadian infantry regiment fought its way across France and Belgium. In October, twenty-five year old Major Chadderton almost died when shrapnel from an exploding German grenade shattered his stomach and legs. Fortunately the collapse of a slit-trench enveloped his injuries, acting as a tourniquet until he was dug from the rubble. One leg had to be amputated.

The former Winnipeger makes his home in Ottawa where he heads War Amps of Canada, chairs the National Council of Veteran Associations and is a director of the Canadian War Museum. Among his many civilian recognitions of achievement, Cliff Chadderton is a recipient of the Order of Ontario (1991) and Order of Canada (1999).

Prologue

Major nations of the world cherish time honored traditions to publicly acclaim feats of conspicuous bravery by their military heroes. This typically involves conferring of a distinctive and colorful medal in a ceremonial rite often centuries old.

For instance Germany's *Pour Le Merite* was established by King Wilhelm I of Brandenberg way back in 1667. At the time French was Brandenberg's official language. Award qualifications were modified by Friedrich the Great in 1740. During World War I the Pour Le Merite was affectionately known as the *Blue Max*. However, this prestigious award ceased to exist with the abdication of Kaiser Wilhelm II in 1918. Germany's top military accolade fell to another medal of long standing, the **Iron Cross** created in 1813 by King Friedrich Wilhelm III of Prussia. During the Second World War the Iron Cross was additionally awarded to uniformed civilian organizations such as police, fire and railroad employees, and to Germany's Axis allies.

France's famous **Legion d' Honneur** was created in 1802 by Napoleon Bonaparte. As well as French citizens, the Legion of Honor is occasionally conferred on France's allies. During the Great War five Canadians were so honored - William Bishop, George MacKay, Donald MacLaren, Redford Mulock, and Ernest Salter.

Contempt for Danger

Italy conceived its *Medaglia al Valore Militare* in 1828. Half a century later Emperor Muts-Hito introduced the *Order of the Chrysanthemum* as Japan's highest military award.

Russia's equivalent is much older. The *Order of Saint Andrew* was instituted in 1698. For fifty years in the 20th Century the St. Andrew was superceded by the *Hero of the Federation* created by the Presidium of the Union of Soviet Socialist Republics in 1939. With the dissolution of the USSR in the 1990s the *Hero Medal* was abolished and Russia, the former USSR's most dominant republic, reverted to the Order of St. Andrew as that nation's highest military award.

The United States of America established the *Medal of Honor* in 1861 to acknowledge individual acts of exceptional bravery by its fighting forces. Since inception, more than 3,400 men plus one woman have been awarded this prestigious honor including more than fifty Canadians. The decoration is often referred to as the Congressional Medal of Honor as the President, in the name of Congress, confers the award.

Until 1993 Canada had no premier military decoration of its own. Instead, the Canadian Government chose to rely on Great Britain as well as other nations to recognize extraordinary military feats exhibited by Canadians. Britain's highest military award, the *Victoria Cross,* is personally or posthumously presented to recipients by Britain's reigning monarch. Queen Victoria presented the first Victoria Cross in an award ceremony on June 26, 1857 involving sixty-two veterans of the Crimean War. Victoria Crosses are fashioned from the bronze cascabels of two Russian cannon captured at Sevastopol; the

Prologue

last great battle of the Crimean War. A cascabel is the large knob at the rear of a cannon used to hold ropes necessary for manhandling the artillery piece. A few years after the medal's inception, new rules were introduced limiting its award to acts of valor occurring only during wartime. Since 1867 the medal has also been awarded to military personnel of Allied forces fighting in the British cause. 1,354 Victoria Crosses have been awarded since its inception.

During the first half of the 20th Century ninety-two Victoria Crosses have been awarded to Canadian military personnel and Canadians serving with another Commonwealth country. There were five Canadian recipients in the Boer War, seventy-one in the Great War, and sixteen in the Second World War.

No one sets out to win a Victoria Cross. It is not a contest. All recipients are ordinary people who, when thrust into an extraordinary circumstance, exhibited common *contempt for danger.* All placed the value of the lives of others before their own.

1
Older Than Canada

The Victoria Cross took root in North America prior to the birth of Canada in 1867. Four recipients - one born in Nova Scotia, one in Quebec and two in Ontario – each earned a Victoria Cross fighting for the British in distant parts of the globe. As well, a British soldier earned his medal of valor en route from Quebec City to Montreal a year before Canadian Confederation.

Alexander Dunn was born in York, Upper Canada in 1833. York reverted to its original name Toronto the following year, and since 1867 the province has been known as Ontario. Alex Dunn was a pupil in Toronto's Upper Canada College when his mother died unexpectedly. Following her death, Alexander and his father moved to England where young Dunn was enrolled in Harrow School. At the age of nineteen Alexander Dunn was commissioned as an officer in the 11th Hussars, a British light cavalry regiment. In 1854 the mustachioed blond-haired Dunn, who stood more than six feet tall, sailed with his unit to Balaclava, a coastal community near Sevastopol in the Crimea. On October 25 six hundred and thirty British cavalrymen charged into a valley heavily defended by Russian troops and artillery. The fateful day was chronicled in Alfred Lord Tennyson's immortal poem, *The Charge of the Light Brigade.* 156

Contempt for Danger

British cavalrymen died that day, 14 were taken prisoner, and another 134 were wounded. Lieutenant Dunn rode with the one hundred and ten troopers of the 11th Hussars. Only twenty-five survived. When the order to retire came, Lieutenant Dunn noticed Russian cavalrymen bearing down on a Hussars sergeant struggling with a severely wounded horse. Wheeling about, Dunn galloped through a maze of dead and dying, and riderless horses charging about from all directions. Slashing and parrying with his saber, Dunn managed to cut down all three of the Russians attacking the sergeant. Dunn dismounted, hefted the sergeant onto his own mount and sent it galloping toward British lines. Lieutenant Dunn next came across a private, also on foot, about to be cut down by a Russian. Dunn killed the enemy attacker then he and the private scrambled toward the British lines.

The Victoria Cross was conceived following the Crimean War and Lieutenant Alexander Robert Dunn was one of its first recipients, and the only officer. His citation reads in part: *For having saved the life of Sergeant Robert Bentley by cutting down three Russian Hussars who were attacking from the rear, and afterwards cutting down a Russian Hussar who was attacking Private Harvey Levett.*

After the war Alexander Dunn quit the army and returned to Toronto bringing with him the wife of a fellow British officer. During the Indian Mutiny of 1857 - 1859, Dunn re-enlisted. At age thirty Dunn became a regimental commander and was the youngest colonel in the British Army. Dunn's regiment served in Malta, India and Abyssinia (now Ethiopia). Colonel

Older Than Canada

Alexander Dunn died of gunshot wounds in Senafe, Abyssinia in 1868. The Toronto born native was only thirty-five.

Herbert Taylor Reade, the son of a surgeon, was born in Perth, Upper Canada (now Ontario) in 1828. Herbert completed undergraduate studies before immigrating to Dublin, Ireland to earn his medical degree. In 1850 Doctor Herbert Reade joined the British Army's 61st Infantry Regiment as an assistant surgeon. During the Indian Mutiny his unit saw action at Ferozepore and the Siege of Delhi. On September 14, 1857 Surgeon Reade was attending to wounded on a Delhi street when they came under fire from rebel snipers on nearby roof tops. Surgeon Reade drew his sword, rallied the few able soldiers in the vicinity, and successfully routed the rebels. His Victoria Cross citation states in part: *The wounded were in very great danger and would have fallen into the hands of the enemy had not Surgeon Reade drawn his sword, and calling upon the few soldiers who were near to follow, succeed under heavy fire in dislodging the rebels.* Reade remained in the army and later became Surgeon General of the Royal Army Medical Corps. The Perth, Ontario hero is buried in Somerset, England.

Billy Hall was born at Horton, Nova Scotia in 1829. At fifteen Billy joined the merchant marine. For the next six years he shipped out of Hantsport, Nova Scotia before joining the Royal Navy in hopes of seeing the world. On November 16, 1857 **Able Seaman William Edward Hall** was a gunner aboard HMS Shannon off the coast near Lucknow, India during the great rebellion. Naval guns had been brought to bear on the Shah Nujeff Mosque in hopes of breaching its walls to enable

Contempt for Danger

British infantry to force a penetration of the stronghold. Indian rebel defenders showered the British ships with a hail of grenades and musket balls causing extensive casualties amongst naval gunners. Seaman Hall and Lieutenant Young were soon the sole survivors of the Shannon's gun crews. Together they continued to load and fire the Shannon's last working gun. Their supreme effort paid off for the wall was breached, allowing British land forces to pour into the mosque and defeat the enemy. Able Seaman William Hall was awarded the Victoria Cross for uncompromising valor. William Hall died at Avonport, Nova Scotia in 1904 at age seventy-five. The inscription on his tombstone describes Hall as the *first man of color to win the Empire's highest award for valor.*

Cam Douglas was born at Gros Ilse, Lower Canada (now Quebec) in 1840. After completing his undergraduate education **Campbell Mellis Douglas** went on to graduate from Edinburgh's School of Medicine in 1861. Doctor Douglas joined the British Army as a surgeon and was attached to the South Wales Borderers Regiment. Surgeon Douglas was with an army unit aboard ship in the Indian Ocean in 1867 when an eighteen man search party was sent ashore at Little Andaman Island to hunt for a naval contingent gone missing. The search party was greeted by a hail of arrows as soon as the men stepped ashore. Scattered human remains on the sandy shore appeared to be the remnants of a British officer and his crew. A violent rain squall suddenly whipped up rendering it impossible for the search party to launch their small boats into the thrashing surf. They were stranded. Frustrated sailors aboard the ship seemed

Older Than Canada

incapable of lending aid to their mates on the beach. Acting on his own initiative Surgeon Douglas took four soldiers in a rescue boat and rowed to shore. It required two attempts and more than an hour to safely negotiate the high rolling surf. In two hazardous trips Douglas and his men picked-up seventeen survivors - a soldier had drowned in the surf - and rowed them back to their ship. All five rescuers were awarded the Victoria Cross.

Doctor Douglas left the British Army in 1882, returned to Canada, and set up medical practice in Lakefield, Ontario. Three years later he joined a Canadian militia expedition ordered to put down a Metis uprising on the prairies. Medical staff and supplies traveled by train to a landing site on the South Saskatchewan River where the steamer Northcote was to carry their two contingents to Saskatoon. Surgeon Douglas was in charge of the second medical contingent. When the Northcote failed to return, Douglas set out by canoe to determine the reason for the delay. Paddling downstream Douglas soon discovered the Northcote aground on a sandbar. Douglas continued his journey, paddling all the way to Saskatoon. He arrived at the village in time to assist in the care of troops wounded at the Battle of Fish Creek. Doctor Douglas remained in Saskatoon to supervise care of the wounded brought from the rebellion's last fire-fight - the Battle of Batoche. Shortly after returning to Ontario, Doctor Douglas decided to immigrate to England. In 1895 daring-do Douglas paddled a canoe named *Saskatoon* across the English Channel from Dover to France.

Contempt for Danger

For his heroic feat in 1866 twenty year old Irishman **Timothy O'Hea** was cited for *conspicuous courage under circumstances of great danger* and awarded the Victoria Cross. O'Hea was one of five British soldiers detailed to guard a boxcar of ammunition being transported by rail from Quebec City to Montreal. Eight hundred German immigrants under medical quarantine were locked in boxcars linked to the ammunition car. When the train stopped at Danville, Quebec on the afternoon of June 9, 1866 Private O'Hea shouted in alarm after noticing the ammunition car was on fire. Fearing an imminent explosion the railroad men and the other four British soldiers fled the scene. Only O'Hea stood fast. Private O'Hea snatched up the keys to the ammunition carriage but could find no means of freeing the human cargo locked in the quarantine-boxcars.

O'Hea frantically tore burning covers from ammunition boxes and hurled them onto the railroad platform. For the next hour he fought the flames with buckets of water he hauled from a nearby creek, cheered-on by hundreds of terrified immigrants locked in the boxcars. Timothy O'Hea single handedly doused the fire. By nightfall, with the ammunition loaded onto another car, the train, including the locked down cars holding the eight hundred German immigrants, resumed its journey to Montreal. The brave British soldier died eight years later in Sturt's Desert, Queensland, Australia.

Older Than Canada

Pre Confederation
Victoria Cross Honor Roll

Surgeon Campbell M. Douglas	**Army**	**Andaman Islands, India 1867**
Lieutenant Alexander R. Dunn	**Army**	**Balaclava, Crimea 1854**
Able Seaman William Hall	**Navy**	**Lucknow, India 1857**
Surgeon Herbert T. Reade	**Army**	**Delhi, India 1857**

2
Birth of a Nation

July 1st 1867 fell on a Monday entitling the public to a rare two day summer holiday. It was a festive occasion. Dawn broke across the land to the peeling of church bells. In countless communities dusk descended amid blossoms of fireworks.

More of Canada's three and a half million people toiled on farms than in any other industry. After agriculture, fishing and logging were Canada's next largest groups. Scarcely fifteen percent of Canadians were employed in manufacturing. Most Canadians were accustomed to working ten hour days six times a week. Canada's largest metropolis, Montreal, was home to 100,000 people. Quebec City had 60,000 people, Toronto 56,000; Halifax and St. John 30,000 each.

Proclamation of the *British North America Act* by Queen Victoria created the *Dominion of Canada*, a nation of just four provinces - Ontario, Quebec, New Brunswick, and Nova Scotia. Ottawa was designated the federal capital.

Despite its vastness, the new country barely constituted 10% of British America's landmass. Ontario, for instance, was but a fraction of its present size. At the time of Confederation Ontario extended north from the Great Lakes to a line running west from the Ottawa River to the head of Lake Superior. East of Ontario, Quebec was a narrow swath of woods and farmland lying astride both sides of the St. Lawrence River before

8

Birth of a Nation

looping southeast to envelop the Gaspe Peninsula. Geographically only New Brunswick and Nova Scotia existed as they do today. Newfoundland, Prince Edward Island, British Columbia and Rupert's Land were not part of Canada in 1867.

Rupert's Land was a five million square mile tract owned by the Hudson's Bay Company. The vast territory extended along Canada's northern border from the Atlantic to Lake Superior, running northward all the way to the Arctic. To the west, Rupert's Land followed the 49th Parallel from Lake Superior to British Columbia, again extending north all the way to the Arctic.

John Alexander Macdonald became Canada's first prime minister when his Conservative Party captured 130 seats in the House of Commons. His government introduced the country's first postage stamp, *the three cent Beaver,* and a brand new Canadian monetary system. For more than one hundred years financial transactions in Britain's American colonies had been transacted in British pound sterling, United States dollars or, in many instances gold. Now all financial dealings in the new Dominion of Canada were to be settled in Canadian dollars.

Britain retained responsibility over international affairs affecting all its holdings in America, including the Dominion of Canada, when it approved the *British North America Act.* London did express its desire that Canada assume responsibility for national defense by backstopping local militia units with a full time army. A seemingly reasonable request, yet it was not to be. A National Defense Bill was introduced in Canada's new Parliament only to be promptly

Contempt for Danger

defeated by Parliamentarians fearing the cost of maintaining a standing army might be excessive for their fledgling nation. There was also a prevalent fear that Britain's insistence on continuing to govern Canada's foreign affairs might, at some point in the future, result in Canadian soldiers being siphoned off to fight distant British battles. Indian troops had recently been ordered to Africa to bolster British forces fighting in Abyssinia.

1867 was also the year the United States of America purchased Alaska from Russia for $7.2 million. The sale prompted the Hudson's Bay Company to offer to transfer ownership of Rupert's Land to the British crown on the understanding Britain would in turn transfer the land to Canada for a fee.

Canada paid the British Government $1.5 million to acquire Rupert's Land. Parliament changed the name of its acquisition to *Northwest Territory*. Canada now extended from the Atlantic Ocean west to the Rocky Mountains, and north to the Arctic seas. On July 15 1870 the Red River community of Selkirk was carved from a sector of Northwest Territory to create *Manitoba*, Canada's fifth province

For forty-two years Manitoba was dogged by the nickname *the postage stamp province* owing to its shape and small geographical size. From 1870 to 1912 Manitoba was a relative oblong approximating Lord Selkirk's original Red River Colony extending from the southern tip of Lake Winnipeg south to the 49th Parallel, and west from Winnipeg to the District of Saskatchewan.

3
Sea to Shining Sea

West of the Rockies the colony of British Columbia flirted with the prospect of joining the Canadian Confederation. Following much debate the British west coast colony finally stipulated its terms for joining the Dominion of Canada.

When Ottawa agreed to all of British Columbia's demands including the construction of both *a transcontinental rail link plus a wagon road* the colony quickly assented. On July 20 1871 British Columbia became Canada's sixth province. Canada now spanned the continent from sea to sea; tucked between three great oceans - the Atlantic, Arctic and Pacific.

One hundred and twelve years following its conquest of Quebec City, British troops finally withdrew from the stone Citadel perched atop the Plains of Abraham. By the end of 1871 the only British forces remaining on Canadian soil were based in Halifax, Nova Scotia and Esquimalt, British Columbia. Primary defense of the Dominion of Canada was coming to rest on Ottawa's shoulders.

Two years later - on July 1, 1873 - Prince Edward Island became Canada's 7th province.

Meanwhile Canada's *rough-and-ready* west remained virtually lawless. The United States brought order to its western territories through the strategic placement of cavalry posts; leaving it up to local communities to appoint county

Contempt for Danger

sheriffs and town marshals. Preferring not to expand its modest-sized army, the Canadian government opted for the creation of a national police force. The *Northwest Mounted Police* was established by Act of Parliament in *1873*. Recruits for Canada's new mounted police service - mostly eastern farm boys and clerks - were attracted west by the prospect of adventure, uniforms and a wage of 75 cents a day. Eight months later the new force announced its first arrests when Inspector *James F. Macleod* and a lone constable took six whisky traders into custody on the south shore of Lake Winnipeg. The following year two hundred and seventy-five Northwest Mounted Police rode seven hundred miles from Winnipeg to the Oldman River near Cypress Hills, District of Alberta where they constructed the NWMP's most western outpost - *Fort Macleod*.

1876 was also the year that *Royal Military College* at Kingston, Ontario was founded. Patterned along the lines of the United States Military Academy at West Point, New York the new college was expected to graduate officers for service in Canada's military.

4
Embracing the West

Quebec's Lieutenant Governor Theodore Robitaille invited Judge Adolphe-Basile Routhier to write the lyrics and Calixa Lavalee the music for a hymn to be played on June 24, 1880 during the St. Jean-Baptiste Day celebrations. The result of their collaboration, Vive la Canadien, was well received by audiences. Re-labeled O Canada in 1901, the popular hymn officially became Canada's national anthem in 1980.

By 1881 Canada's population had risen to 4,325,000; almost equally divided between male and female. Ontario with 1,925,000 people had the largest population; Quebec at 1,360,000 was second. British Columbia with 49,000 had the least number of people. Persons of French descent represented the largest ethnic segment; those of Irish descent came second, English settlers ranked third. Montreal's population of *140,000* remained much larger than Toronto's *86,000.*

Each year thousands of newcomers trudged through Winnipeg, Manitoba - *Canada's Gateway to the West.* Most were immigrants fresh from Europe.

The Metis, being part native, part French, were long time settlers of the region lying just west of Selkirk, Manitoba. Prior to Confederation the Metis had sought annexation by the United States. Now, in 1885, they sought independence from Canada. To further their aims the Metis established a

Contempt for Danger

provisional government at Batoche, Northwest Territory and declared their independence. White settlers neared panic when the Metis began to arrest local officials and clergy; really anyone in authority who dared publicly disagree with the rebellion. Ottawa was advised of the uprising through the newly installed telegraph system. The government hurriedly dispatched five thousand militia from Ontario under command of British Army General Frederick Middleton. General Middleton's orders were to put down the rebellion and quell native uprisings, particularly those orchestrated by the Cree.

Growing frustration over alleged government mismanagement had nudged the Cree and Stoney tribes into a loose alliance with the Metis in their rebellion against Canada. *Chief Poundmaker* a forty-three year old Cree chieftain was revered by his people as a visionary and great hunter.

The army quickly defeated the Metis but not before their native allies killed a federal Indian Agent, two priests and six settlers at *Frog Lake*, Northwest Territory. Native warriors also kidnapped two of the slain men's wives as well as a priest and a Hudson's Bay Company employee. Middleton's troops launched a vigorous search for the Frog Lake captives who miraculously were found alive. Reverend Charles Quinney and Hudson's Bay Company employee Bill Cameron were freed when discovered in the company of a small band of Cree warriors. Two days later Theresa Delaney and Theresa Gowanlock escaped their captors.

Cree and Stoney warriors did win some skirmishes against the Canadian militia yet within a month Chief Poundmaker

Embracing the West

was compelled to surrender to General Middleton at Battleford. The rebellion was over.

Upon their return to Ontario General Middleton and his *Dominion Troops* were feted as heroes. Each militiaman received a silver medal in recognition of their participation in Canada's first troop action.

The nation's first transcontinental railroad was officially opened with a ceremony at Eagle Pass, British Columbia in November of 1885. *Donald Smith*, senior director of the Canadian Pacific Railway (CPR), and Sandford Fleming participated in the historic event. Fleming, the designer of Canada's first postage stamp, was also noted for drafting an alternative route for the CPR and conceiving the concept of *standard time zones* used to this day throughout the world. Although taking 10-1/2 years to complete, the historic railroad opened five years ahead of schedule.

Canada's 1891 census recorded a population of 4,835,000. The city of Montreal was still the nation's largest metropolis with 217,000 residents; Toronto recorded 181,000 people, Quebec City 63,000.

Province	Population
British Columbia	98,000
Northwest Territory	99,000
Manitoba	153,000
Ontario	2,115,000
Quebec	1,490,000
New Brunswick	320,000

Contempt for Danger

Nova Scotia	450,000
Prince Edward Island	110,000
National	4,835,000

In 1892 Great Britain authorized Canada to fly a *Red Ensign* as its national symbol. The basically red banner featured a Union Jack in the upper left fly, with Canada's coat-of-arms positioned to the right. The following year Governor General Lord Stanley presented the Montreal Amateur Athletic Association with a trophy bearing his name. Since 1893 the *Stanley Cup* has been awarded to the season's champion hockey team.

In 1895 the northern portion of Northwest Territory was lopped off at the 60th Parallel and divided into four provisional districts - Yukon, Mackenzie, Ungava and Franklin. Land below the 60th Parallel (later to become Alberta, Saskatchewan and northern Manitoba) was named Athabaska Territory.

Thousands of fortune-seekers rushed to Yukon District in 1897 following announcement of a gold strike. The following year Yukon's status was elevated from District to Territory. That summer thirty thousand visitors passed through Dawson City, Yukon Territory. Really only a town, Dawson City was a rough frontier community featuring fine wines and the latest fashions from New York and Europe. The Northwest Mounted Police were called upon to patrol its muddy streets and surrounding environs.

Embracing the West

Meanwhile across the seas Britain publicly expressed concern for the safety of Her Majesty's subjects and possessions in South Africa before unilaterally annexing the republic of Transvaal. The *Boers* – Dutch residents of the Transvaal and the Orange Free State - revolted. Full scale war broke out in the autumn of 1899.

5
Canadian Expeditionary Force

Canada acquiesced to Britain's request for military assistance in the South Africa campaign after the British publicly aired an offer to fund the entire cost of a Canadian Expeditionary Force once it arrived in South Africa. Canada declined Britain's financial incentive by quickly agreeing to fully finance the cost of Canadian military expeditions overseas.

Inside of a month a thousand young men volunteered for one year's service with the Canadian Expeditionary Force - *for Queen and Country*. They were to serve in the specially created Second Infantry Battalion of the *Royal Canadian Regiment*. Formed in 1883, the RCR was Canada's first permanent army regiment. It first saw action suppressing rebel forces in 1885 at Batoche, Saskatchewan and Cut-Knife Creek. In 1898 the RCR was assigned to preserve Canadian sovereignty in Yukon Territory during the gold rush frenzy. Now it was assuming an overseas responsibility; a first for the Canadian Army.

The raw recruits were issued uniforms, kit and rifles, organized into platoons, transported by train to Quebec City and marched directly aboard a waiting ship - all within three weeks of enlistment. *Lieutenant Colonel William D. Otter* was their commanding officer. Otter was a veteran militiaman cited

18

Canadian Expeditionary Force

for leading a successful charge against Cree defenders in the 1885 Northwest Rebellion.

RCR's 2nd Infantry Battalion was accorded a tumultuous sendoff at Quebec City. Cheering throngs lined the wharves. Thousands more rooted from the Plains of Abraham, the escarpment overlooking the harbor. Still more well-wishers cheered from flotillas of small craft and commercial shipping. Crowds cheered and waved vigorously as the troopship slowly cleared Quebec harbor.

Onlookers had no way of knowing the SS Sardinia, a converted cattle steamer, was ill equipped for its task as troop carrier. It took Sardinia thirty grueling days to lumber 7,000 miles to Cape Town, South Africa. Soldiers slept in cots and hammocks nested in every available nook of the hold with their gear tucked alongside them. Drinking water was so scarce it had to be rationed, and water spigots guarded by armed sentries. Finally, on November 29 1899, the Sardinia docked at Cape Town. The men received a month's pay upon arrival and were given twenty-four hours liberty in the South African city.

Two days later the Canadian Expeditionary Force (CEF) boarded trains destined for Belmont, northeast of Cape Town. The torrid South African summer near devastated the new arrivals from the northern hemisphere. Daytime temperatures routinely approached 115 degrees Fahrenheit. At Belmont the Canadians were given less than thirty days basic infantry training before being thrown into battle on New Year's Day 1900.

Contempt for Danger

Second Battalion, RCR, fought its most significant battle at Paardeberg. They were outnumbered by a well dug-in Boer force.

Twenty-three year old Irish-Canadian **Richard Rowland Thompson**, a medical orderly attached to D Company was at Paardeberg. On the night of February 18th Private Thompson crept from the safety of his trench to offer aid and comfort to a badly wounded infantryman abandoned on the battlefield. He saved the life of the injured Canadian. Ten days later Thompson slithered into the night on several occasions and again at great risk to himself provided aid to suffering infantrymen stranded in the dangerous stretch of no-man's land separating Canadian and Boer battle lines. Thompson was twice nominated for the Victoria Cross. And twice his case was *not recognized* - military parlance for rejected in favor of another candidate. However, that summer a most prestigious and unique award was conferred on Private Richard Thompson - *The Queen's Scarf of Honor.*

Queen Victoria personally crocheted several woolen scarves, each bearing a silk embroidered Royal Cipher. The ceremonial scarf was intended to be worn as a sash extending from the right shoulder diagonally across the torso and cinched to the wearer's waist on the left side. Four crocheted scarves were allocated to the British Army and one to each of the Dominions fighting with British forces in South Africa. To qualify, candidates had to have been cited for extraordinary bravery, must be of *other ranks* (British parlance for enlisted men) and must have previously been nominated for the

Canadian Expeditionary Force

Victoria Cross but *not recognized.* 2nd Battalion, RCR was the only Canadian fighting unit in South Africa at the time and RCR officers submitted the name of Private Thompson. In the summer of 1900 Thompson was presented with his Scarf of Honor. Richard Rowland Thompson died in 1908 at age 31 and is buried at Chelsea, Quebec. His Queen's Scarf of Honor, the only such award ever presented to a Canadian is on display at the Royal Canadian Regiment Museum in Ottawa.

February 27th 1900 was a meaningful day for Private Thompson and the men he rescued. It was also the day that Boer commander General Cronje surrendered his forces to the victorious RCR's 2nd infantry battalion.

2nd Battalion was involved in many skirmishes following the two month Battle of Paardeberg. In April Lieutenant Colonel Otter, the battalion's commanding officer, was felled by rifle wounds to his neck and chin. Otter subsequently recovered and was able to resume command of his battalion.

William Otter was born in Clinton, Canada West in 1843. He fought with the militia against Fenian renegades in 1866. He joined the Canadian Army in 1883 and two years later led a column against rebel forcess in the Northwest Rebellion. In 1908 Major General Otter was appointed the first Canadian-born chief of the general staff in Ottawa. During the Great War General Otter was placed in charge of enemy internment. William Otter died in Toronto, Ontario in 1929, at age eighty-six.

While fighting in the Boer War as part of the British 19th Brigade the Canadians were often in the vanguard. The

Contempt for Danger

19th marched three hundred miles in eighty-three days - skirmishing almost continuously with the Boers as they retreated northward.

Owing to the lack of an effective materiel replenishment program, the CEF was obliged to improvise as best it may. Troops were unable to change their clothing for weeks on end. Dogged by heat, dust, thirst, lice - even a plague of locusts - uniforms turned to rags, underwear disintegrated, leather boots wore out. Desperate Canadian troops scavenged remnants of military and civilian garb wherever it could be found, including from the dead of both sides. Some of the infantry wore overcoats with nothing beneath. Yet the record shows the battalion's bedraggled appearance never diminished Canadian fighting capacity.

In March of 1900 three fast ships from Halifax offloaded additional Canadian troops and 1,200 horses. The second contingent of the Canadian Expeditionary Force had arrived. It comprised two cavalry battalions from the *Royal Canadian Dragoons* - a unit from the Army's permanent force plus a battalion of new recruits. In addition, there were three batteries of *Royal Canadian Artillery* - about 900 men. Meanwhile, back in Canada, a third overseas contingent was being organized.

The third contingent was a cavalry troop designated the *Lord Strathcona Horse*. The Strathcona regiment was funded by wealthy Canadian industrialist Donald Smith who had made his fortune investing in Canadian Pacific Railway. It was Donald Smith who had ceremoniously driven the final spike at Eagle Pass in 1885 officially opening Canada's first

Canadian Expeditionary Force

transcontinental railroad. Smith later served as president of the Bank of Montreal. In recognition of his contribution to the Empire, Queen Victoria bestowed on Smith the title Lord Strathcona. Smith was Canada's High Commissioner (ambassador) to London when he announced his decision to fund a Canadian cavalry troop to fight in the Boer War. With approval from the War Department in Ottawa, Smith named Samuel Steele as his cavalry troop's first commanding officer.

6
Sam Steele

Samuel Benfield Steele was born in Purbrook, Canada West (now Ontario) in 1849. Orphaned at age 13, Sam enlisted with the local militia at age sixteen. Sam Steele was one of the earliest volunteers for the Northwest Mounted Police (NWMP) when it was formed in 1873. With the NWMP Steele fought against Fenian marauders and participated in quelling the Northwest Rebellion of 1885. Sergeant-Major Steele was cited for his *strength, determination, character and commitment*. In 1887 Sam Steele established Kootenay Post, the first NWMP command west of the Rockies - a huge responsibility. Kootenay's raucous saloons were popular hangouts for tough railroad construction workers and hard-rock miners. To maintain order over his rough-and-ready precinct Sam organized *Steele's Scouts*; an amalgam of twenty-five Mounties plus one hundred Alberta cowboys and frontiersmen.

Twenty-nine year old Marie Elizabeth Harwood entered Sam Steele's life in 1889. Marie came from a wealthy Montreal family. Her father was a Member of Parliament. That summer Marie was the guest of the wife of a NWMP superintendent stationed at Fort McLeod. Marie's friends introduced her to the Fort's famous thirty year old commander Samuel Steele. Within months they were husband and wife. Sam and Marie had two

Sam Steele

daughters and a son when, in 1898, he was dispatched to Dawson City to restore order in the Klondike goldfields. Marie and the children moved to Montreal.

In September of the following year when Superintendent Steele was relieved of his responsibilities in Dawson City he immediately joined his family in Montreal. Sam might well have thought his days of adventure were over before Donald Smith invited him to assume command of a newly formed cavalry outfit destined for the Boer War in South Africa.

When Sam accepted Smith's invitation to recruit and train the new cavalry regiment he was given the rank of lieutenant colonel by the Canadian Army. With Stetson hats canted at a jaunty angle, Steele and his five hundred rough riders shipped off to South Africa. Unfortunately most of their horses failed to survive the long ocean voyage and the Strathconas were obliged to retrain on Argentinean ponies before engaging in battle.

Despite the openly critical attitude often displayed by British officers toward *colonial troops*, a British general remarked "There is no better commander than the rough-riding colonel from Canada." Indeed, one of Steele's troopers, Sergeant Arthur Richardson, became the first Canadian in the South African campaign to be awarded the Victoria Cross.

Sam Steele was restless for more adventure after bringing his cavalry troop back to Canada. The Boer War was still raging and it didn't take long for him to decide to accept an invitation to return to South Africa as head of a military police division. He returned to his family when the war ended.

Contempt for Danger

He was sixty-five years old when the Great War broke out in 1914. Sam Steele, probably Canada's most well known soldier at the time, was given the rank of major general and placed in charge of overseeing the combat readiness training program for Canadian Expeditionary Forces arriving in Britain. Sam's family joined him and remained with him throughout the war. Although General Steele retired from the army in the summer of 1918, he and his family chose to remain in London until the new year. An epidemic of influenza raged through Europe causing thousands of deaths and Sam succumbed to the dreaded illness. Samuel Benfield Steele died in London on January 30 1919, at the age of 69; having devoted a lifetime in the service of his country. He was honored by a military service in London attended by Northwest Mounted Police and Army contingents. Six Canadian Army generals served as pall bearers. In accordance with his wishes Canada's gallant hero was subsequently interred in Winnipeg, *Gateway to the West* as Sam always thought of the Manitoba capital.

7
The Boer War

Arthur H. L. Richardson was born in Liverpool England in 1873. At age twenty-five Art Richardson immigrated to Canada, taking work as an Alberta ranch hand before joining the NWMP. Arthur knew of Sam Steele by reputation and was quick to enlist in the newly formed Lord Strathcona Horse cavalry. Sergeant Richardson earned his Victoria Cross on July 5, 1900. Richardson was in the company of thirty-seven other cavalrymen when they encountered a Boer force more than twice their number. A firefight ensued. Richardson disregarded the bugler's call to withdraw and instead rode directly into withering enemy fire to rescue a badly wounded trooper whose horse had been shot out from under him. Richardson's steed was hit as it charged, yet the wounded horse did not falter. Richardson scooped his comrade up onto the injured mount and galloped to safety. Years after the war Arthur Richardson returned to his native England where he died in 1932 at age 59.

William Henry Snyder Nickerson, born in Canada in 1875, received his education in the British Isles. In 1898 twenty-three year old Nickerson enlisted in the Royal Army Medical Corps and became a career medical officer. He earned his Victoria Cross April 20, 1900 at Wakkerstroom, South Africa while infantry units were advancing in support of the cavalry.

Contempt for Danger

Lieutenant Nickerson exposed himself to extremely heavy shell and rifle fire to care for a wounded soldier. He remained with the suffering soldier until he could be safely removed from the battlefront. William Nickerson remained in the Royal Army, latterly as Director of Medical Services, India until his retirement in 1933. Called back from retirement in 1939, General Nickerson served with the British Home Guard during World War II. William Nickerson is buried in Kintyre, Scotland.

Toward the end of their one-year enlistment Canada's soldiers were withdrawn from battle and shipped home. The first contingent to return was the 2nd Infantry Battalion, RCR. Upon arrival in Halifax they were outfitted with new uniforms before boarding a train to participate in a victory parade in the nation's capital. When men of the 2nd Infantry Battalion, Royal Canadian Regiment, were released from active service, the battalion was disbanded.

By November 1900 the Boers need for heavy weapons had become critical. To ease the situation they hit upon the idea of capturing Canadian guns in the Komati River area by mounting surprise attacks. Suddenly thrust into a battle for their lives Canadian Dragoons and Canadian Artillery units made a spirited stand to save their batteries from capture. In the process, three troopers of the Canadian Dragoons Regiment were cited for extreme bravery and earned a Victoria Cross for their actions of November 7th - Lieutenant Hampden Cockburn, Lieutenant Richard Turner, and Sergeant Edward Holland.

The Boer War

Thirty-two year old *Lieutenant Hampden Zane Churchill Cockburn* hailed from Toronto. On November 7th his unit was under siege and his platoon had been cut down to a handful of troopers. Nevertheless they were the only unit in a position to prevent Boers from capturing a Canadian artillery emplacement. Following several unsuccessful frontal attacks, the Boers backed off to search for easier prey. The enemy apparently failed to realize that Lieutenant Cockburn and all his remaining men were wounded. One more push, even a slight one, may well have taken the battery. Lieutenant Cockburn recovered from his wounds and remained in the army, subsequently attaining the rank of major.

Lieutenant Richard Ernest William Turner was 29 years of age when he arrived in Africa. On the morning of the 7th he noticed that a nearby Canadian artillery battery was at risk of being captured. Ignoring the agony from two bullet wounds, Lieutenant Turner dismounted and deployed his troopers at close quarters. They repelled the enemy several times and the artillery remained in Canadian hands. Turner enjoyed army life and remained in the service. During the Great War of 1914 - 1918 he attained the rank of Lieutenant General and at one point commanded all Canadian forces stationed in Great Britain.

Twenty-two year old *Sergeant Edward James Gibson Holland* had only his Colt revolver to rout attacking Boers intent on capturing a Canadian artillery gun carriage harnessed to a dead horse. Sergeant Holland dismounted and raced to the field gun and unfastened the weapon from its carriage.

Contempt for Danger

Summoning all his strength, the sergeant manhandled the gun from its carriage and waddled off with it to his frightened horse. Miraculously he was able to remount and, with the gun cradled in his arms, galloped to safety. Edward Holland also chose to remain in the army following the war and was subsequently commissioned as an officer; eventually attaining the rank of major.

Lieutenant Colonel Steele's Strathcona Horse regiment, being the last to arrive in South Africa, was the final contingent of the Canadian Expeditionary Force to ship back to Canada. Figuring that a rigorous sea voyage would be too much for their horses, the Stathconas left their Argentinean ponies in South Africa.

Canada's Expeditionary Force had been composed almost entirely of English-speaking volunteers. Most French-speaking Canadians refused to fight in what they termed *a British war*. While English-speaking supporters argued that all of Canada should respond to the British Empire's plea for assistance, Quebecers for the most part insisted Canadians ought to be *more nationalistic* in spirit. They argued that the Boers never posed a threat to Canada nor was survival of the British Empire ever in jeopardy.

Apart from Quebec, most of Canada at the beginning of the 20th Century was pro-British in spirit. To most it seemed important, if not critical that member nations of the British Empire collaborate in a military federation. To this day main streets of many major communities in English-speaking Canada bear such names as Queen, Victoria, Albert, or King.

The Boer War

Of the 8,300 Canadian troops who rotated through South Africa, 135 lost their lives. Another 252 were wounded. Canada's troops had long since returned home by the time the Armistice was signed on May 31, 1902 officially ending the war.

Boer War
Victoria Cross Honor Roll

Lieutenant Hampden Z. C. Cockburn	Army	Komati River, South Africa 1900
Sergeant Edward J. G. Holland	Army	Komati River, South Africa 1900
Lieutenant William H. S. Nickerson	Army	Wakkerstroom, South Africa 1900
Sergeant Arthur H. L. Richardson	Army	Wolwespruit, South Africa 1900
Lieutenant Richard E. W. Turner	Army	Komati River, South Africa 1900

8
An Exciting New Century

Eighty-one year old Queen Victoria died January 22nd 1901. Scarcely four years earlier Her Highness celebrated her Diamond Jubilee - sixty years on the British throne.

1901 was also the year that Montreal based Merchants Bank changed its name to Royal Bank of Canada. In December the world's first Trans Atlantic wireless message was transmitted from England to twenty-seven year old Guglielmo Marconi perched atop Signal Hill overlooking Newfoundland's capital city of St. John's.

Vaudeville acts and musical shows were the pinnacle of entertainment at the turn of the century. Moving pictures - silent, short, black and white movies - began to appear in nickelodeons and luminieres. As movie viewing increased in popularity, theater owners added musical accompaniment and hired scene describers to excite the audience.

On the streets horse drawn trolleys plied main thoroughfares. The increasing number of automobiles and trucks appearing on city streets heightened public demand for paved roads. Inter urban transportation was still the almost exclusive domain of railroads and their steam powered locomotives.

By 1905 the city of Winnipeg had emerged as the largest grain-handler in North America, processing almost sixty

An Exciting New Century

million bushels a year. On September 1st of that year Athabaska Territory was carved in two to create Canada's eighth and ninth provinces - Alberta and Saskatchewan. Alberta was named in honor of Queen Victoria's fourth daughter, whereas Saskatchewan is Cree for *the river runs smoothly.*

Downtown San Francisco was virtually destroyed by fire following a violent earthquake in 1906. It was also the year that British troops vacated Esquimalt, British Columbia leaving the Royal Navy base at Halifax, Nova Scotia as the sole British military installation in Canada.

The Ottawa Senators ice hockey team won the 1909 Stanley Cup. That fall the University of Toronto overcame Toronto Parkdale Canoe Club to win Canada's annual football classic. Governor General Earl Grey was in attendance to present the victorious team a large silver cup bearing his name - the *Grey Cup.*

Passage by Canada's Parliament of the Naval Service Bill in 1910 established the Canadian Navy. The Act envisaged Canada's navy being placed under British command in the event of war. To help launch this new marine venture Canada purchased an 11,000 ton battleship plus one cruiser from the Royal Navy. The Canadian Government also established a college in Halifax to graduate future naval officers. Course material and tests were set out by the British Admiralty.

Canada was steadily becoming more industrialized. The nation was already recognized as an agricultural producer of world significance. Wheat production had ballooned to a record seventy-five million bushels a year. The latest census

Contempt for Danger

placed Canada's population at 7.2 million people. Cities were flourishing, particularly those in the west. In a single decade Vancouver's population mushroomed from 25,000 to 100,000; Calgary from 5,000 residents to 75,000; Edmonton from 4,000 to 60,000; Regina from 2,000 to 30,000; Saskatoon from 100 residents to 12,000; Winnipeg from 40,000 to 140,000.

During the night of April 15, 1912 RMS Titanic, the world's largest and fastest passenger liner, struck an iceberg off the coast of Newfoundland on her maiden voyage from Southampton, England to New York City. The huge liner sank with great loss of life.

The following month the provincial boundaries of three provinces were significantly expanded. Manitoba now extended north from the United States border all the way to the 60th Parallel, the same latitude as Saskatchewan and Alberta. Ontario now lapped the shores of Hudson's Bay, and Quebec abutted the Arctic and Atlantic Oceans.

In September 1912 huge crowds cheered a spectacular hour-long parade of cowboys, native peoples, pioneers, and mounted police at the opening of the first Calgary Stampede. The inaugural event was organized by Guy Weadick and his trick horse riding wife Flores Ladue.

The first class of cadets graduated from Halifax's new Naval College in 1913. In central Canada the five hundred foot, 5,000 ton James Carruthers, the largest freighter ever built in the British Empire, was launched at Collingwood, Ontario.

9
Call to War

The *Great War* was triggered by the assassination of Archduke Franz Ferdinand, heir to the Austro-Hungarian Empire, and his wife by a Serbian nationalist in Sarajevo, Bosnia. Their murders occurring on June 28, 1914 led to a war pitting France, Russia and Serbia against Germany and her Austro-Hungarian allies. Britain might well have remained out of the conflict had Germany not invaded neutral Belgium. Great Britain honored its 1839 mutual defense pact with Belgium by declaring war on Germany.

Both sides employed innovative weapons and tactics in what would eventually become a worldwide conflagration - trench warfare, poisonous gasses, tanks, flamethrowers, magazine loading rifles, machineguns, rapid-fire artillery, bomb-laden inflatable airships, and airplanes. Within four years ten million people would perish.

For Canada the Great War commenced with Britain's declaration of hostilities against Germany. Canada was automatically drawn into the fray by virtue of its membership in the British Empire. The only decision the Canadian government had to make was how much to contribute to the war effort.

Contempt for Danger

In the spring of 1914 Canada's militia consisted of 3,100 regulars and 75,000 partially trained reservists. Recruits were paid $1.10 per day and soon almost 100,000 Canadians volunteered for *king and country*. Canada's lone battleship sailed from Halifax with a crew of seven hundred to join the Royal Navy on the other side of the Atlantic. In Esquimalt, British Columbia the navy's other capital ship, a cruiser, was placed on stand-by. To augment its small fleet the Canadian Navy purchased two submarines from the United States.

French offensive action against the Germans in the first two weeks of war fizzled out when the enemy launched a multi-pronged counterattack. Sweeping through Belgium and northern France, the German Army came within artillery range of Paris. In October the British engaged the Germans in a pitched battle at Ypres, Belgium. Within weeks a stalemate extended across the entire Western Front - from the North Sea to Switzerland. Both sides developed intricate and complex trench systems behind a front that would remain virtually unchanged until the spring of 1917. Both sides battered away at seemingly impenetrable defenses to no avail. With casualties numbering in the hundreds of thousands the sacrifice of life and limb reached unparalleled proportions.

Lance Corporal Michael O'Leary of 1st Battalion, Irish Guards Regiment, British Army was the first Canadian in the Great War to be awarded a Victoria Cross. O'Leary's unit stormed enemy barricades on February 1, 1915. Being a fast runner, O'Leary made a headlong dash toward the enemy, easily outpacing his comrades. He killed five Germans en route

Call to War

to the first barricade. Scarcely pausing, O'Leary attacked a second barricade some sixty yards further on, capturing it, killing three of the enemy and taking two Germans prisoner. The rapid, clear thinking action of twenty-six year old Lance Corporal Michael O'Leary prevented others in his unit from being fired upon. Michael O'Leary remained in the army, subsequently becoming a commissioned officer, eventually attaining the rank of major.

The first wave of Canada's Expeditionary Force sailed from Halifax to Britain in the fall of 1914. In England, Canada's thirty-one thousand untrained soldiers were placed under command of Lieutenant General E. A. Anderson, Royal Army.

Many Canadian civilians were amongst the twelve hundred lost at sea when a German submarine torpedoed the British luxury liner Lusitania off the coast of Ireland. Eight years earlier Lusitania had achieved a Trans Atlantic crossing speed record of four days, nineteen hours.

Concerned with the loyalties of European immigrants, the Canadian government decreed that all recent arrivals from Germany, Austria, Hungary and the Ukraine must register with the authorities and carry special government-issued identification. Later, many thousands of so called *enemy aliens* were interned in the twenty-four concentration camps the government established across Canada.

10
Ypres, Belgium

By mid January 1915 *1st Canadian Division* had taken up position north of Armentieres, France. The Canucks immediately came under fire. Twenty-four days later 1st Division was withdrawn from the line, refitted, and ordered to Ypres.

German military forces had completely overrun Belgium the previous summer, except for one small sector - a salient jutting from France into Belgium. The previous autumn, the Germans vigorously tried to dislodge the salient's stubborn British defenders in what has since been described as *the first Battle of Ypres.*

Ypres is nestled in a West Flanders' valley between the Yser and Lys Rivers. High ground on three sides of the salient teemed with deeply dug-in Germans. While Ypres was the principal town in the salient other communities, such as Kerselaere and Saint Julien, lay nearby. Defense of the salient made little sense militarily. It was largely for political reasons the Allies were so determined to hang on to this isolated shred of Belgium territory.

1st Canadian Division moved into the Ypres defense lines on April 15th. One week later the Canadians participated in a major British offensive - *the Second Battle of Ypres*. Time and again Canada's infantry leapt aggressively over the top of their trenches into withering enemy fire. When the Allies fell back,

Ypres, Belgium

enemy artillery lobbed *poisonous gas* filled canisters into their positions. Exploding canisters spewed chlorine gas over Allied entrenchments. Vapors, hovering at ground level drifted down into crevices - especially trenches and shell holes. Inhaling chlorine caused the victim's lungs to quickly swell, resulting in an agonizing death by suffocation. It was the first time in history that deadly respiratory gasses had been used in battle. Unsuspecting and unprepared Allied troops, including Canadians, were the first victims of an enemy gas attack.

Over-the-top charges into heavily defended enemy lines took a terrible toll of lives. German defenses were invariably protected by coils of barbed wire entanglements, with machineguns positioned every few hundred feet. And, everywhere there was mud. Troops by the thousands of both sides died charging enemy defenses. The hiatus between over-the-top charges was peppered by explosions from heavy artillery and mortars. Many helplessly wounded soldiers drowned in water-filled shell holes.

Canada's infantry sustained six thousand casualties the first week of battle on the Ypres front. Among the dead lay *Lieutenant Cameron Brant*, a direct descendant of onetime Six Nations leader Joseph Brant. After witnessing the carnage at Ypres, Canadian medical officer Lieutenant Colonel **John McCrae** was inspired to pen his famous poem *In Flanders Fields*.

Four Canadians were awarded the Victoria Cross for heroism at Ypres - Lance Corporal Fred Fisher, Lieutenant Ed Bellew, Sergeant Major Fred Hall, and Captain Frank Scrimger.

Contempt for Danger

Lance Corporal Frederick Fisher was a machinegun squad-leader with 13th Battalion, Royal Highlanders (Quebec) Regiment. At St. Julien, Belgium on April 23, Fisher advanced with his squad under heavy fire to cover the withdrawal of a Canadian gun battery. The battery was saved but four of Fisher's men died in the process. Later the same day Fisher, assisted by four replacements, led another advance under heavy fire. This time 20 year old Fred Fisher was killed in action. His Victoria Cross was awarded posthumously.

Ed Bellew was born in Bombay, India in 1892. He immigrated to Canada in 1907, settling in British Columbia. When war broke out Ed joined the 7th Battalion, British Columbia Regiment and within months was shipped overseas. On April 24th 1915 Lieutenant Bellew, a machinegun platoon officer, was embattled near Kerselaere, Belgium. His platoon had brought an enemy unit to an abrupt halt. Lieutenant Bellew re-positioned two of his machineguns just as the enemy attacked in force. Canadian reinforcements sent to Bellew's aid were quickly surrounded by the enemy and killed. With no help in the offing, Bellew's platoon was soon reduced to himself and Sergeant Peerless. The two desperate Canadians elected to fight it out. They maintained fire until their ammunition ran out. Sergeant Peerless was killed and Lieutenant Bellew was wounded. The thirty-two year old lieutenant smashed-up his one remaining machinegun, grabbed a rifle and was still fighting when taken prisoner. He was held in captivity by the Germans until 1919. Victoria Cross recipient Edward Donald Bellew subsequently attained the rank of captain.

Ypres, Belgium

Born in Kilkenny, Ireland *Fred Hall* came to Canada when he was twenty-five, taking up residence on Pine Street in Winnipeg. Pine Street is possibly the only street in the world to have produced three Victoria Cross recipients; the other two being Leo Clarke and Robert Shankland. Fred Hall was a Company Sergeant Major serving with 8th Battalion, 90th Winnipeg Rifle Regiment. On April 24, 1915 during the battle of St. Julien near Ypres a wounded Canadian infantryman lay moaning in no-man's land about fifty feet beyond the Canuck line. Any discernable movement in the Canadian trenches immediately attracted a furious spate of enemy fire. Yet the thirty year old company sergeant-major was determined to retrieve his fallen comrade. Hall's first attempt to do so was unsuccessful. On his second try Hall made it to the side of the wounded man unscathed. As he lifted the wounded soldier from the ground Sergeant Major Frederick William Hall was struck in the head with a sniper's bullet. His Victoria Cross was awarded posthumously.

Francis Alexander Caron Scrimger was the medical officer for 14th Battalion, 3rd Brigade, Montreal Regiment, 1st Canadian Division. The thirty-five year old captain was born in Montreal in 1880, earning his medical degree at McGill University twenty-five years later. On the afternoon of April 25, 1915 Captain Scrimger was in charge of an advanced dressing station housed in a stable at St. Julien when an order was received to withdraw from the area. The farm buildings were under heavy fire as Captain Scrimger directed the removal of the wounded. Captain Scrimger hoisted the last wounded

Contempt for Danger

officer onto his shoulder and carried him toward safety. When he was unable to carry the officer any further, Captain Scrimger lowered him to the ground and remained at the wounded man's side until help arrived. His Victoria Cross citation reads in part: *During the very heavy fighting between 22nd and 25th April Captain Scrimger displayed continuously day and night the greatest devotion to duty among the wounded at the front.* Francis Alexander Caron Scrimger subsequently attained the rank of lieutenant colonel. Doctor Scrimger died in 1937, age 57.

Before hostilities began Ypres had been a peaceful town of tree lined streets cozily nestled in a hollow. After innumerable artillery bombardments the pretty Belgian community was pulverized to rubble and dust. The sole discernable remnant in the town square was the shell of a building known as Cloth Hall. Ypres has since been restored, and is now a city. Menin Gate is the Ypres Memorial to Commonwealth Soldiers. Every night since the memorial was unveiled in 1927 a bugler has sounded the Last Post - the only exception to this ritual occurred during the German occupation of Belgium in World War II.

Not far from Ypres, at St. Julien, stands an impressive Canadian War Memorial - the *Brooding Soldier*. The stone monument depicts a helmeted infantryman in battledress, head bowed, rifle at reverse arms, bayonet aimed downward. The scene's simplicity implies sorrow while expressing thoughts of sacrifice.

Lieutenant Frederick Campbell was born in Mount Forest, Ontario in 1867. He fought in the Boer War with 30th Battalion,

Ypres, Belgium

Wellington Rifles. In September of 1914 Campbell shipped overseas with 1st Battalion, Western Ontario Regiment. At Givenchy, France on June 15, 1915 Lieutenant Campbell was advancing under heavy fire with two of his machinegun detachments. When almost all of his gun crews were killed or wounded, Campbell still forged ahead. He reached the German front line trench with only one gun still firing. When the Germans counterattacked, Lieutenant Campbell and Harold Vincent, who had stuck with his lieutenant, waded into the advancing enemy lugging their last machinegun. Campbell fired over one thousand rounds from a machinegun strapped to the back of Vincent, a former lumberjack. The enemy faltered then dispersed under the Campbell/Vincent onslaught. Vincent was badly burned from the heat generated by the gun yet survived. Forty-eight year old Lieutenant Fred Campbell was mortally wounded and died four days later. His Victoria Cross was awarded posthumously. Frederick William Campbell is buried at Boulogne, France.

11
The Somme, France

In the early stages of the war Canada's citizen soldiers were shipped overseas poorly equipped. Their greatcoats absorbed water rather than repelling it. Combat boots disintegrated under battlefield conditions. Leather gear chafed and tugged uncomfortably. Entrenching tools were cumbersome and inefficient. The Canadian Army's standard issue weapon, the Ross Rifle, was unreliable and dangerous.

The *Ross Rifle* was designed for hunters by Scottish born Charles Ross. It functioned well when used by snipers, but the Ross was grossly unsuitable for infantry. The absence of tempered steel in critical areas caused the Ross to jam frequently and occasionally explode. Even its bayonet had a tendency to fall off when jostled. Canada was two years into the war before most substandard equipment was replaced.

Captain John Alexander Sinton was a 31 year old Irish/Canadian serving with the Indian Army Medical Corps stationed in Mesopotamia. Captain Sinton, who had demonstrated his bravery in battle on three prior occasions, earned his Victoria Cross for actions on January 21, 1916. While attending to wounded in his care, his battalion aid station came under heavy enemy fire. Bullets pierced both of Captain Sinton's arms. He was also wounded in the side. Despite his injuries Captain Sinton refused to be evacuated and, although

The Somme, France

almost disabled, he continued to minister to other casualties. John Sinton survived and remained in the army long after the war ended. Eventually John Sinton attained the rank of brigadier general.

In the spring of 1916 one thousand four hundred Canadians were killed in the Battle of the Craters at St. Eloi, France. At Mount Sorel, another eight thousand Canadian casualties were sustained in hand-to-hand fighting.

Twenty-two year old Canadian *Tom Wilkinson* was a lieutenant with 7th Battalion of the British Army's North Lancashire Regiment. On July 5, 1916 when the 7th came under attack Lieutenant Wilkinson observed a group from another unit retreating without taking their machinegun. Wilkinson and two of his men took over the abandoned British machinegun, and opened fire into advancing Germans at point blank range. To his left Wilkinson noticed Germans hurtling grenades over a dirt mound where five confused British soldiers lay huddled. Toting the abandoned machinegun under his arm, Lieutenant Wilkinson forced his way forward, crawled atop the dirt mound and opened fire causing the enemy to flee. Lieutenant Wilkinson was shot and killed just after scooping up a wounded comrade he hoped to carry to safety. Thomas Orde Lauder Wilkinson was awarded his Victoria Cross posthumously.

Machineguns were the technological marvel of ground warfare. The German Army favored water-cooled heavy machineguns to thwart Allied advances. For much of the first two years of the Great War, standard Allied methods for

Contempt for Danger

dislodging an entrenched enemy were *over the top standing shoulder to shoulder* charges. Wave upon wave of infantrymen relinquished the relative safety of their trenches to wade across barren landscapes into the cross-fire of strategically positioned enemy machineguns. Thousands of dutiful troops were slaughtered in this gruesome fashion, yet attackers seldom enjoyed any significant degree of success. When pressed, German defenders temporarily withdrew to pre-dug secondary or tertiary defense lines until the Allied push waned.

Eventually Allied offensive tactics were modified. In addition to night reconnaissance missions, an increasing number of bomber units were being sent out. Bombers were small units of armed men lugging as many hand grenades as they could tote. To destroy machinegun posts and other fortifications, bomber units had to creep close to enemy trenches before lobbing their grenades. Soldiers knew that every machinegun eliminated significantly increased their chance of survival. Such knowledge inspired an increasing number of individuals to try to destroy enemy machinegun posts.

By the summer of 1916 the Canadian Expeditionary Force had grown to Corps size, embracing three divisions totaling some 90,000 troops. In September the new *Canadian Corps* was ordered from Ypres to the Somme sector and placed under command of British Lieutenant General Julian Byng

The battlefront straddled the River Somme from Beaumont-Hamel in the north to far beyond Maisonette in the south. Gazing across no-man's land Canadians saw three lines of

The Somme, France

German defenses, each protected by two thirty foot coils of barbed wire. The lunar-like landscape was a monochrome of sun dried mud, offering few hints civilization had ever existed. Wreckage from the few still visible trees and buildings were caked with dust and mud. Wooden planks straddled the mire of muck. Stagnant water oozed through the mud in the base of trenches and myriad of dugouts that were the homes of troops and vermin. Yet the pervasive putrid stench seemed noticeable only to new arrivals.

The Battle of the Somme lasted 142 days - from July through mid November 1916. In the end the Allies had gained a mere 125 square miles of additional territory at horrendous cost - 625,000 casualties; 415,000 of whom fell under British command. The opening battle was preceded in late June by a week long artillery barrage from 1,600 British field guns against German positions. On July 1st one hundred and ten thousand British-led troops went over the ramparts, wading into the German defenses. Less than half the attackers survived - 19,000 died in action, almost another 40,000 were wounded or went missing in action. For almost two weeks following the initial assault British forces continued to sustain an average of ten thousand casualties a day.

Canadians back home were rocked by a particularly grim report from the Somme. The *Newfoundland Expeditionary Force* had been annihilated. Although Newfoundland was still a British colony, Canadians felt affinity with their Maritime neighbors. Prior to their transfer to the battlefronts of northern Europe the Newfoundland Regiment had fought with

Contempt for Danger

distinction at the Battle of Gallipoli. The NEF was decimated at Beaumont-Hamel, France on July 1st - the opening day of the Battle of the Somme. Only 68 Newfoundlanders survived the nightmare. Yet within months a re-staffed re-equipped NEF rejoined the battle.

Canadian Corps joined the Battle of the Somme on September 15th, 1916 the same date the British introduced their latest innovative weapon - tanks. In their first week of battle the CEF suffered 7,200 casualties.

In the two months that the CEF fought at the Somme - mid September through November - Canadians suffered 24,000 casualties. Of the many Canadians cited for bravery during those brutal days, three were awarded the Victoria Cross - Corporal Leo Clarke, Private Chip Kerr, and Piper Jim Richardson.

Leo Clarke was a 23 year old corporal serving with 2nd Battalion, Eastern Ontario Regiment. Before the war Leo lived on Pine Street in Winnipeg, Manitoba. The city later changed the name of Pine Street to Valour Road when it was discovered that three Victoria Cross recipients had lived on the street. On September 9, 1916 near Pozieres, France Corporal Clarke and his unit were guarding the construction of a modification to a recently captured trench when they were attacked by a German platoon. Clarke emptied his revolver firing at the attackers. He then picked up two enemy rifles to continue his defense. A German officer wounded Clarke with a bayonet. Clarke shot him dead then continued to chase the enemy, shooting four more. Corporal Clarke's Victoria Cross had to be awarded

48

The Somme, France

posthumously because ten days later he was killed in action at Etretat, France.

Private John Chipman Kerr was born in Fox River, Nova Scotia in 1887. He went overseas with the 49th Battalion, Alberta Regiment. On September 16, 1916 twenty-nine year old Chip Kerr was the designated *bayonet man* assigned to protect a bomber unit prowling close to German trenches. When the unit began to run low on grenades, Private Kerr was dispatched to get more. Kerr chose to walk along the *pardos* - the dirt embankment behind a German trench intended to protect those in the trench from attack from the rear. Trudging along the pardos Kerr startled a company of German troops. Without hesitation Kerr opened fire. He charged along the pardos yelling, weaving and ducking; all the time firing round after round at point blank range. In the darkness the stunned Germans thought they had somehow become surrounded by a superior Canadian force. Unaware they had been confronted by a lone Canadian soldier they promptly surrendered. In the heat of battle two of Chip Kerr's fingers had been shot off. Quickly wrapping his wounded hand in a dirty rag Kerr took charge of 62 surrendering Germans plus a thousand feet of enemy trench works. Private John Kerr wasted no time marching his glum faced prisoners to the Canadian lines and captivity. He died in 1963, age 76. Mount Kerr in Jasper National Park is named in his honor.

Jim Richardson, a Canadian of Scot descent, was a Piper with 16th Battalion, Manitoba Regiment. Richardson's company was attempting to creep through the enemy's

Contempt for Danger

barbed-wire defenses when intense fire stalled them in their tracks. Richardson grabbed his bag-pipes, wangled through the wire and stood erect on the German side of the line. There Piper Richardson proceeded to parade back and forth continuously playing the tune *Over The Top*. Jim Richardson's impulsive bravery inspired men in his unit to rush the wire and successfully capture their objective. Later the same day Piper Richardson was escorting a wounded comrade plus some German prisoners toward the rear when he was killed. Twenty year old Piper James Cleland Richardson was awarded his Victoria Cross posthumously. He is buried at Adanac Military Cemetery northeast of Albert, France.

In mid October of 1916 newly arrived Canadian 4th Division moved into the line to replace the diminished Canadian Corps. The remnants of Canadian Corps - 1st, 2nd and 3rd divisions - were withdrawn from the Somme and ordered north to a place called Vimy.

12
Ridge of Death

By 1917 the Canadian government no longer attempted to mask the fact the war was going poorly. Canada had sent 300,000 troops overseas with a promise of two hundred thousand more. To spur recruiting, enlistment standards were amended to enable the army to accept native peoples, Afro-Canadians, Asians and marginal medical risks.

Canadians at home really had no conception of life in the trenches - its lice, or the mites. Or the barbed wire. Or the stench of feces, urine, blood and rotting corpses. For most, enlistment was simply electing to do *the right thing*.

In a patriotic gesture residents of the then small southern Ontario city of Berlin changed the name of their community to Kitchener in honor of the famous soldier and British Minister of War. General Kitchener, a Boer War hero, was lost at sea in the current war when the Royal Navy destroyer conveying him to Russia was sunk off the coast of Scotland.

Ontario followed in the footsteps of the four western provinces in February 1917 by extending the voting franchise to women. In April of 1917 the United States Congress declared war on Germany.

Canada's Expeditionary Force held a four mile sector of the front west of Vimy, France. On the southern flank was 1st

Contempt for Danger

Canadian Division. 2nd Division came next, then 3rd Division. 4th Division held the northern most slot. British troops anchored both Canadian perimeters; Britain's 51st Highland Division covered 1st Division's right flank, British First Corps was dug-in to the left of 4th Canadian Division.

The CEF was expected to advance to a line running from Givenchy in the north to Farbus in the south. The city of Vimy lay almost dead center of the target line. However, the real challenge lay in securing a fifty foot high ridge separating the Canadians from their objective - Vimy Ridge. The Ridge had been an enemy stronghold since 1914 and the deeply entrenched German troops and artillery had good reason for believing their position was impregnable.

French attempts to retake Vimy Ridge faltered before ceasing altogether after the French Army suffered 150,000 casualties. British attempts to assail the Ridge also ended in failure. The Ridge's defenders calmly and confidently observed the Canadian troops massing in the plain below. They knew their enemy was Canadian from the increasing frequency of skirmishes fought in recent weeks.

The CEF aligned fifty regiments and battalions along the Vimy front. Some of the more well known units to fight at Vimy were:

Black Watch (42nd Montreal)

Canadian Scottish Regiment (16th BC)

Canadien Francais (22nd Montreal)

5th Royal Highlanders (Montreal)

48th Highlanders Regiment (Toronto)

Ridge of Death

Grenadier Guards (87th Montreal)

Jolly 75th (75th Mississauga)

Lord Strathcona Horse

Princess Patricia's Canadian Light Infantry

Little Black Devils (8th Winnipeg)

Royal Canadian Regiment (Toronto)

Royal Montreal Regiment

Royal Regiment of Canada (3rd Toronto)

Seaforth Highlanders (72nd Vancouver)

Tobin's Tigers (29th Vancouver)

Victoria Rifles (24th Montreal)

Warden's Warriors (102nd BC)

Canadian troops had few idle moments in the weeks preceding the upcoming battle, popularly rumored to begin on the Easter weekend. Miners from Nova Scotia dug tunnels beneath no-man's-land leading toward the Ridge. Other troops constructed wide-access trenches to facilitate rapid transport of reserves and ammunition once the attack began. In the relative safety of the rear, troops drilled, practiced assaults and defense against gas attack. Everyone down to platoon level was instructed in their respective objectives; target, positioning, timing - until then a virtually unheard of degree of troop edification. Between maneuvers, Canadian units continued to harass the Germans. Indeed, in the final two weeks prior to the major assault the CEF suffered almost 1,700 casualties.

Contempt for Danger

Victoria Cross recipient *Thain MacDowell* was born in 1890 at Lachute, Quebec. He moved to Maitland, Ontario as a youth and joined the army after graduating from university. In 1915 he was a captain in the 38th Ottawa Battalion. On April 9 1917 twenty-six year old Captain MacDowell and two of his men captured two enemy machineguns intact. They also captured seventeen Germans including two officers. Despite suffering a hand wound, Captain MacDowell held the former enemy position for five days before being relieved by his battalion. Thain Wendell MacDowell later attained the rank of colonel. He died at his Brockville, Ontario home in 1960, at age seventy.

The same day that Captain MacDowell earned his Victoria Cross *Bill Milne*, a twenty-four year old private with 16th Battalion, Manitoba Regiment and his unit were tied down by deadly fire from a German machinegun. Acting on his own initiative Private Milne crawled forward to the machinegun nest, killed the shooters and captured the gun intact. Incredibly, Private Milne repeated the feat later that same day. William Johnstone Milne's Victoria Cross had to be awarded posthumously as he was killed in action shortly after the repeat performance.

Ellis Sifton was a member of 18th Battalion, Western Ontario Regiment. On April 9th Sergeant Sifton's unit was flayed by machinegun fire while attacking enemy trenches. Twenty-five year old Ellis charged the machinegun nest and killed its crew. At that point Sergeant Sifton was attacked by other Germans filing into the nest from an adjoining trench. Using his rifle Sergeant Sifton bayoneted and clubbed the

Ridge of Death

enemy trying to kill him. The sergeant's ferocity held the enemy at bay until help arrived. Sifton's rescuers saved the captured machinegun nest but not their sergeant. Ellis Welwood Sifton had been fatally wounded.

Private **John Pattison** served with the Alberta Regiment. On April 10th a German machinegun inflicted heavy losses on Pattison's unit. On his own initiative the forty-one year old Calgarian sprang forward, racing from shell hole to shell hole until he was within ninety feet of the machinegun nest. Hurling grenades, he killed and wounded several Germans. He then charged the nest, bayoneting five of the enemy. John George Pattison was awarded his Victoria Cross posthumously after being killed in a separate action on June 3 near Lens, France. Mount Pattison in Jasper National Park is named in his honor.

At 5:30 am Easter Monday, April 17, 1917 the Canadian Expeditionary Force launched its attack on Vimy Ridge. Heavy artillery pounding the Ridge kept the Germans hunkered down. Assault waves from Canada's four divisions went over-the-top into no-man's land as well as beneath it through tunnels burrowed earlier by the Nova Scotians. A relentless battle ebbed and flowed for several days. Eventually Canadian assault forces overwhelmed the German defenders. Vimy Ridge was theirs. In six days of fighting the CEF sustained 11,000 casualties - 3,600 killed, 7,000 wounded, 400 missing in action. Four thousand Germans were taken prisoner. Canadian troops had achieved what many said was impossible.

13
Hill 70

Although the battle for Vimy Ridge was over, the fighting was not.

Lieutenant Rob Combe was a company commander with 27th Battalion, Manitoba Regiment. On May 3, 1917 the Winnipegger led his company on a *bomber mission* through intense fire. Only Combe and five of his men reached their objective where they lobbed grenades at the enemy, inflicting multiple casualties. Other Canadians joined Lieutenant Combe to help his bombers assault an enemy fortification. They captured their objective and took eighty German grenadiers prisoner. Lieutenant Combe assembled a second bomber unit and immediately set off on another mission. They were driving the enemy back when Robert Grierson Combe was killed by a German sniper. His Victoria Cross was awarded posthumously.

In the summer of 1917 Major General Arthur Currie, commander of 1st Canadian Division, was promoted to lieutenant general and placed in command of the entire Canadian Corps. Currie now held the most senior position ever held by a Canadian in the field of battle. General Currie successfully led the Canadian Expeditionary Force in their attack of Hill 70 near Lens, France; a strategic follow through to the Vimy Ridge triumph.

Hill 70

Arthur Currie was born in Napperton, Ontario in 1875. Soon after moving to Victoria, British Columbia seventeen year old Art Currie joined the militia. When the Great War broke out Currie had already risen in rank to lieutenant colonel. In 1914 he was given command of 2nd Infantry Brigade based at Valcartier, Quebec. A year later Currie was appointed commander of 1st Canadian Division. Major General Currie was heavily involved in the planning of the battle for Vimy Ridge. Now as a lieutenant general, Currie successfully commanded Canadian Corps until war's end. British Prime Minister Lloyd George described Currie as brilliant, and one of the best corps commanders in the British Forces. After the war Arthur Currie headed McGill University from 1920 until his death in 1934.

Hill 70 is located between Cite St. Auguste and Loos. It was not as high as the ridge at Vimy, yet it was the high ground confronting 1st Canadian Division. The division attacked Hill 70 on August 15 1917, meeting with stubborn resistance almost from the outset. Three days later the Germans counterattacked, using flame throwers in attempts to clear the parapets of its Canadian defenders. Canadian soldiers Harry Brown, Fred Hobson and O'Kill Learmonth were there.

Harry Brown, only nineteen years old, was a private with 10th Battalion, Alberta Regiment. Following the capture of an enemy position at Hill 70 the Germans counterattacked in force. Within a short time the Canadians found themselves in a critical situation. When their signal wires were severed,

Contempt for Danger

Private Brown and another soldier were ordered to get an important message through to the Canadian main line.

The other messenger was killed and Brown's arm was shattered. In great pain Private Harry Brown struggled to achieve his objective. He was successful but died of his wounds. Victoria cross recipient Harry Brown is buried near Lens, France.

Fred Hobson was born in London, England in 1873. He served with 2nd Battalion, Wiltshire Regiment during the Boer War. After immigrating to Canada he married a Galt, Ontario storekeeper named Louise. Fred was employed by Canadian Canners in Simcoe, Ontario when the Great War commenced. In November 1914 he joined up and was wounded at the Battle of the Somme two years later. On August 17, 1917 Fred Hobson was a forty-three year old sergeant serving with 20th Battalion, 1st Central Ontario Regiment. That morning the regiment was engaged in repelling an enemy counterattack at Hill 70. Sergeant Hobson was keeping an eye on a forward positioned Canadian machinegun when a shell-burst killed all its crew but one, and buried the gun in the earth. Sergeant Hobson leapt from the relative safety of his trench, rushed forward and dug the machinegun from the rubble. Although he was not a trained machine gunner Hobson was able to get the weapon to fire. But when it jammed he left the gun to the sole surviving crew member and rushed forward alone. With his rifle Hobson bayoneted and clubbed the advancing enemy until felled by the impact of a German bullet. By this time the Canadian machinegun was again firing and continued to do so until

58

Hill 70

reinforcements arrived to repel the Germans. Regrettably, the relief unit arrived too late to save the sergeant. Frederick Hobson was awarded his Victoria Cross posthumously.

Twenty-three year old *Major O'Kill Learmonth* was with 2nd Battalion, Eastern Ontario Regiment when he received a Military Cross after being wounded at Ypres. Now Learmonth's battalion was under attack at Hill 70. When some of his men recoiled at the onslaught, Major Learmonth lobbed grenades at their attackers. Despite the pain from two wounds, he inspired his men to counterattack. The Germans were repulsed. Later during an intense barrage Major Learmonth was wounded a third time. Despite his wounds he stood resolutely astride a trench parapet hurling grenades at the enemy. On several occasions he was able to catch a German hand-grenade and toss it back. Bleeding profusely he fell to the ground, unable to maintain the fight. Major Learmonth broke his leg when he fell into the trench yet continued to direct his company from where he lay. Before being evacuated the major insisted on giving a complete briefing to his second in command. Although mortally wounded, Major Learmonth instructed his stretcher bearers to take him to battalion headquarters in order to personally apprise them of the situation. Major O'Kill Massey Learmonth died in the dressing station and was awarded his Victoria Cross posthumously. The major is buried near Lens.

Two other Victoria Cross recipients at the Battle of Hill 70 were Irish/Canadians from Burnaby, British Columbia - Private Mike O'Rourke and Sergeant Major Bob Hanna.

Contempt for Danger

Private Mike O'Rourke was a stretcher bearer with 7th Battalion, British Columbia Regiment. In mid August, thirty-nine year old O'Rourke labored unceasingly for three days and nights retrieving wounded from a battlefield swept by machinegun and rifle fire and bombarded by enemy artillery. O'Rourke dressed wounds and administered food and water. On several occasions he was knocked to the ground and partially buried by exploding artillery shells. His Victoria Cross citation said *Private Michael James O'Rourke's demonstration of courage and devotion in carrying out his rescue work in spite of exhaustion and incessant heavy fire, inspired all ranks and undoubtedly saved many lives.*

The other Irish/Canadian hero from Burnaby, B.C. was *Company Sergeant Major Bob Hill Hanna* of 29th Battalion, British Columbia Regiment. On September 21 Sergeant Major Hanna's company was attempting to take a heavily defended enemy strong point at Lens. All the company's officers had been knocked out of action during three previous attempts to achieve their objective. Yet thirty year old Hanna rallied his remaining men and led them on a fourth attempt. They stormed the machinegun post, killing its German defenders and capturing the gun intact. Robert Hanna was later promoted to lieutenant.

Filip Konowal was another brave Canadian soldier to earn a Victoria Cross at Lens. Recalling the event many years later Konowal remarked: *'I was so fed up standing in the trench with water to my waist that I said the hell with it and started after the German Army,'* adding *'My captain tried to shoot me because he*

Hill 70

figured I was deserting.' Filip was born in 1888 at Kudkiv, Ukraine, then part of the Russian Empire although his Canadian Army enlistment papers indicate his birthplace as Redeski, Russia. While serving in the Imperial Russian Army Filip married a young Ukranian named Anna. After fulfilling his five years service, Filip left the Russian Army to immigrate to Canada in 1913, intending to send for Anna and their daughter Maria once he became established in the new land. However, his plans were dashed when war erupted in Europe the following year. Filip enlisted in the Canadian Army in 1915 and shipped overseas with 77th Battalion. In France he was transferred to British Columbia Regiment's 47th Battalion.

On August 22, 1917 Corporal Konowal was placed in charge of a section ordered to mop up enemy pockets in cellars, craters and machinegun emplacements in the vicinity of Lens. Approaching his task with zeal, Corporal Konowal's unit inflicted heavy casualties. On several occasions the corporal attacked enemy emplacements single-handedly. Once, he entered a gun emplacement alone, killing the German crew and capturing their machinegun intact. The following day he personally blew up another gun emplacement. Within three days all resistance had been successfully overcome. Corporal Konowal was severely wounded when struck by a sniper's bullet. While recouperating in an English hospital bed with half his face shot off Filip Konowal was personally awarded his Victoria Cross by King George V who said: *'Your exploit is one of the most daring and heroic in the history of my army. For this, accept my thanks.'*

Contempt for Danger

Following his recovery Corporal Konowal was temporarily assigned to assist the Military Attaché at the Russian Embassy in London. Toward the end of the war Konowal, now a sergeant, was transferred to the hastily created Canadian Siberian Expeditionary Force and shipped to Vladivostok. He and his unit returned to Canada in June of 1919.

Filip Konowal headed the first Peace Parade in Ottawa on July 1st 1919. The next day tragedy struck. Filip Konowal killed a man in Hull, Quebec following an altercation. While details of the incident remain sketchy, Filip Konowal was incarcerated in a Montreal mental health facility for six years. In 1928 Major Milton Gregg, another VC recipient, came across Konowal and was able to secure a job for him as a cleaner in the House of Commons. Shortly after Konowal's plight was brought to the attention of Prime Minister MacKenzie King, Filip Konowal was appointed chief custodian of the *Speaker's Room* in the Prime Minister's Office.

Filip learned that his wife Anna and daughter Maria had died in the Soviet Ukraine during the genocidal Great Famine of 1932-33. In 1934 Filip married Juliette Leduc-Auger. Twenty-five years later the Canadian war hero died peacefully at age seventy-two. The Canadian War Museum was in possession of Konowal's Victoria Cross when the medal went missing. For more than a quarter of a century its whereabouts were generally unknown. Then in 2004 a tip received from Iain Stewart, of England, alerted Professor Lubomyr Luciuk at Kingston's Royal Military College that the medal was headed for the auction block in London, Ontario. Luciuk's quick action

62

Hill 70

led to the recovery of Filip Konowal's Victoria Cross by the RCMP. Subsequently the medal was returned to the Canadian War Museum at a ceremony that August. In his memory Canadian Legion Branch Number 360 in Toronto is named in Filip Konowal's honor.

Shortly after taking Hill 70 Canadian Corps commander Lieutenant General Currie shifted his troops north. His Canadians were about to join the bloody see-saw battle that had been raging all summer at Passchendaele.

14
Passchendaele, Belgium

The first Battle of Ypres was fought in 1914. Canadian troops fought in the second Battle of Ypres the next spring. The Third Battle of Ypres got underway July 31, 1917 and did not end until November 10th.

General Currie was told by British commander Field Marshal Douglas Haig that the Allies needed a victory in Flanders to bolster sagging British and French morale. The British had suffered appalling losses. Worse, apart from believing their efforts may have blunted some of Germany's ability to continue the war, no material gain had been achieved. Not only was the French Army experiencing a similar lack of success elsewhere along the front, it had to contend with mutinous factions in sixty of its one hundred and ten divisions.

Canada was ordered to take Passchendaele, a village on the far side of a ridge. Ypres had been virtually destroyed in the preceding battles. The entire Ypres front was synonymous with a sea of mud - actually more like a thick, oozing mass of thigh-high brown porridge. August rains had become double the rainfall of the previous year. Successive heavy artillery barrages had wrecked the sewage and drainage systems. In low lying marsh areas the front was almost impenetrable. It took up to eight struggling soldiers to manhandle a single stretcher

Passchendaele, Belgium

bearing a wounded comrade across the quagmire. Supplies were short and there was little drinking water; certainly none for bathing. Yet water was all around; in flooded trenches, in dug-outs, even swirling through washed-out latrine pits. Putrid, odorous, brackish water filled thousands of shell holes that pockmarked the grim terrain.

Phil Bent grew up in Halifax, Nova Scotia. In 1907, at age sixteen, young Phil enlisted as a naval cadet and served two years aboard HMS Conway, a sailing ship of the British Navy used for training. Following his stint aboard the Conway, Phil became a merchant seaman. He had almost earned his Merchant Navy Officer Certificate when war was declared. Phil was anxious to get into action and since contemporary views suggested the war might end before Christmas Phil and a buddy signed up with a Scottish regiment. Philip Bent soon made his mark in the British Army. Within three years he rose to the rank of lieutenant colonel in the Leicestershire Regiment and was already entitled to wear the Distinguished Service Order medal. On October 1st, 1917 near the Polygon Wood sector of the Ypres front, Bent's regiment came under intense artillery and machinegun fire. Lieutenant Colonel Bent took a reserve platoon and, together with remnants of several other companies already in the line, led a successful counterattack. Regrettably he was killed leading the charge. Philip Eric Bent's Victoria Cross citation said this of the twenty-six year old officer from Nova Scotia: *The coolness and magnificent example of the colonel resulted in the securing of a portion of the line essential to subsequent operations.*

Contempt for Danger

To reach their objective with minimal troop loss Canadian planners knew they had to move rapidly across the mire of no-man's land. General Currie envisioned a network of corduroy wood roads strung across the mud flats similar to those he had seen in northern Ontario. Currie's novel concept was not known to have been previously tried in warfare with the result that the British high command was reluctant to approve his plan. Eventually Currie's plan was authorized. Since wooden planks were unavailable, the CEF built a sawmill, cut down fresh timber, and made their own rough hewn planks which they laid out in a series of *one-way routes* to and from the front. Although squishy, the corduroy roads supported the movement of horses and wagons, artillery, troops and materiel. The concept worked! From then to the end of the war the viability of employing corduroy log roads was an option taken into consideration in future attacks.

On October 18, 1917 the Canadian Expeditionary Force launched its major offensive, a battle that raged until November 10th.

Tom Holmes from Owen Sound was a private with the Canadian Mounted Rifles, 2nd Central Ontario Regiment. On October 26th the right flank of Holmes' unit was held up by devastating fire from a German pillbox. The Canadian Rifles sustained heavy casualties. The situation had become critical. On his own initiative Private Holmes dashed forward and with two accurately thrown hand grenades nullified two machinegun crews sharing the same pillbox. When Holmes hurled another grenade into the entrance of the pillbox,

Passchendaele, Belgium

nineteen frightened Germans surrendered. Thomas William Holmes was only nineteen years of age when he earned his Victoria Cross.

Two other Canadians earned a Victoria Cross at Passchendaele that day - Chris O'Kelly and Bob Shankland. Both were westerners.

Chris O'Kelly was a twenty-one year old captain with 52nd Battalion, Manitoba Regiment. Captain O'Kelly led his company with *extraordinary skill and determination*, advancing more than 1,000 yards across open land without benefit of covering fire. As they advanced, his company knocked out six enemy pillboxes, took one hundred prisoners and captured ten enemy machineguns. O'Kelly's company nabbed even more prisoners while repelling a German counterattack. That night they captured an enemy reconnaissance party, taking eleven Germans including an officer prisoner. In a separate action Christopher Patrick John O'Kelly earned the Military Cross. Later he attained the rank of major. After the war O'Kelly tried his hand at prospecting near Ear Falls, Ontario. In 1922 Chris O'Kelly drowned while canoeing on Lake Seul, Ontario when caught in a sudden rain squall. He was twenty-six.

Another officer, *Lieutenant Robert Shankland* served with 43rd Battalion, Manitoba Regiment. During a fierce battle Lieutenant Shankland rallied the remnants of his platoon and rounded up pockets of men from other platoons. His expert deployment enabled his troops to inflict heavy losses as the enemy fled. After repelling the German counterattack Lieutenant Shankland slipped back to brigade headquarters to

Contempt for Danger

personally report his observations. Shankland promptly returned to his advance post and remained there until relieved. Robert Shankland was the third resident of Pine Street in Winnipeg to be awarded the Victoria Cross. The other two Pine Street residents were Sergeant Major Fred Hall and Corporal Leo Clarke. In commemoration of the trio's heroic achievements the city of Winnipeg changed the name of Pine Street to Valour Road. Bob Shankland went on to serve in World War II, eventually retiring as a lieutenant colonel. Robert Shankland died in 1968, age 80.

Cecil Kinross was born in Stirling, Scotland in 1896. His family immigrated to Alberta in 1912 and settled on a farm near Lougheed. Three years later Cecil Kinross joined the army. The westerner was a twenty year old private with the 49th Battalion, Alberta Regiment when his unit was held up on October 30th by murderous machinegun fire. Shucking all his equipment save his rifle and bandolier, Private Kinross advanced alone across open ground toward the chattering machinegun. He charged the emplacement, killed its crew of six, and destroyed the machinegun. Cecil Kinross' *superb example and courage enabled a highly important position to be established.* Following his return to Canada in 1919 Victoria Cross recipient Private Kinross was feted to a gala reception at the Pantages Theater in Edmonton. In 1951 Mount Kinross near Jasper, Alberta was named in his honor. Cecil John Kinross, a lifelong bachelor, died in Lougheed in 1957. He was sixty-one.

George Mullin was born in Portland, Oregon in 1892. He immigrated to Canada and enlisted in the 28th Infantry

Passchendaele, Belgium

Battalion. In March 1915 Private Mullin transferred to the Princess Patricia's Canadian Light Infantry regiment already entrenched at the front. Two months later George Mullin made corporal, and in June of 1916 was promoted to sergeant. He was awarded his Victoria Cross for actions at Passchendaele on October 30, 1917. His citation reads in part: *Sergeant Mullin performed the incredible feat of taking the pill box single-handed. He rushed a sniper post in front and destroyed the garrison with grenades and crawling on top of the pill box, shot the two machinegunners with his revolver. Sergeant Mullin then rushed to another entrance and compelled the garrison of ten to surrender. His gallantry and fearlessness was witnessed by many and although rapid fire was directed in his direction, he not only helped to save the situation but also indirectly saved many lives.* George Mullin was promoted to lieutenant and later attained the rank of major. Following the war George Mullin elected to remain in Canada. He died in Regina, Saskatchewan in 1964, age 72.

Born in Liverpool, England in 1885 **Hugh McKenzie** immigrated to Canada at a young age. When war broke out he enlisted in the Princess Patricia Canadian Light Infantry. In January 1917, while serving with 7th Machinegun Company, he was promoted to lieutenant. Ten months later on October 30th, Lieutenant McKenzie led a section of four machineguns in support of an infantry attack near Meetscheele Spur, Belgium on the Passchendaele front. The infantry faltered when all their officers and most of their non-commissioned officers lay dead or wounded. Lieutenant McKenzie turned his machinegun unit over to his next in command and rushed to rally the infantry.

Contempt for Danger

He organized an attack on enemy fortifications and captured them. Lieutenant McKenzie then led a successful attack against an enemy pillbox. Thirty-one year old Hugh McKenzie was killed in this action and his Victoria Cross was awarded posthumously. He was also a recipient of France's Croix de Guerre.

George Randolph Pearkes was born in Watford, England in 1888. After finishing school he and a brother immigrated to Red Deer, Alberta. George Pearkes resigned from the Northwest Mounted Police to join the army in 1915. On October 30, 1917 Pearkes was a major with the 5th Mounted Rifle Battalion, Quebec Regiment when he suffered a wound in his right thigh. Ignoring the pain Major Pearkes continued to direct his men in their defense of a key position. Pearkes was wounded four more times while successfully repelling multiple enemy counterattacks. His Victoria Cross citation said twenty-six year old Major George Randolph Pearkes *showed supreme contempt of danger and wonderful powers of command and leadership*. George Pearkes remained in the army, later attaining the rank of major general. He also earned a Distinguished Service Cross and the Military Cross. After leaving the army in 1945 George Pearkes became a Member of Parliament. Following a stint as Canada's Minister of Defense, George Pearkes served as British Columbia's Lieutenant Governor. George Pearkes retired to Victoria and for the next ten years, 1966 - 1976, served as president of the Canadian Legion.

Jimmy Robertson was born in Nova Scotia in 1883. At sixteen he moved to Medicine Hat, Alberta taking a job with

Passchendaele, Belgium

Canadian Pacific Railway. Jimmy was a thirty-two year old locomotive engineer when he joined the army in 1915. Jimmy Robertson shipped overseas with 27th Battalion, Manitoba Regiment. On November 6, 1917 Robertson's platoon was held up by enemy machinegun fire in the battle for Passchendaele. On his own initiative Jimmy Robertson rushed the gun, killed four of its crew and turned the machinegun on the Germans. He then picked up the gun, and with his platoon at his heels, raced to a forward position where he used the German machinegun to inflict many more casualties. His actions enabled the rest of his company to consolidate and advance further. Private Robertson saw two wounded Canadians lying on the ground. He crawled to their assistance and managed to carry one safely back to the rear. He was in the process of picking up the second wounded soldier when he was shot and killed by a sniper's bullet. Private Robertson was awarded his Victoria Cross posthumously. James Peter Robertson is buried at Tyne Cot Cemetery, Passchendaele, Belgium. He was 34.

Corporal Colin Barron, a twenty-four year old Scottish/Canadian from Toronto, was also awarded a Victoria Cross for bravery that day. Colin was with 3rd Battalion, 1st Central Ontario Regiment when his platoon got held up by three German machineguns. After taking stock of the situation the corporal rushed toward the guns, opening fire at point blank range killing four of the German crew. The rest surrendered. Corporal Barron inflicted numerous casualties when he turned one of the guns on the retreating enemy.

Contempt for Danger

Colin Fraser Barron's bravery and success enabled 3rd Battalion to make a significant penetration of the German line.

German defenders in the village of Passchendaele succumbed to the Canadian onslaught. Four days later the Third Battle of Ypres was over. The victors of Vimy Ridge had given the Allies the victory they hungered for, but at a cost. During the month that Canadian Corps was in the Passchendaele line almost 16,000 casualties were sustained.

Conscription finally came to Canada in the summer of 1917 with the passing of the Military Services Act (MSA). The MSA obliged all men between ages 20 through 45 to register with their local draft board. Voters in eight of Canada's nine provinces voted in favor of conscription with only Quebec voting against. Yet the draft was by no means universally popular. Riots broke out in Quebec when police attempted to arrest draft dodgers. In one incident four civilians were killed and five soldiers injured. For awhile Quebec jails were crammed with protestors. Protests elsewhere were generally more subtle.

Parliamentarians were rattled upon learning that ninety percent of the 400,000 national draft registrants had applied for exemption. This caused the MSA to bog down because the Act required pleas for exemption to be adjudicated individually by local tribunals. Public reaction shook the government's resolve and the draft was implemented very slowly. When the first call-up came in October 1917 draftees were told not to report until January. It then took until mid

Passchendaele, Belgium

spring of 1918 before the first draftees arrived overseas. In the end less than 25,000 draftees ever reached France.

In January 1918 a 5th Canadian Division was in Britain, trained and ready to form up with the Canadian Expeditionary Force. However, in light of the dismal response to recruiting efforts 5th Division was deactivated. Its troops were urgently required elsewhere and were funneled into Canadian Corps' existing four divisions to cover shortfalls in ranks.

15
War in the Air

It had been scarcely a decade since two Ohio bicycle mechanics, Wilbur and Orville Wright, completed the world's first airborne flight at Kittyhawk, North Carolina. The brothers actually undertook four flights December 17, 1903; the longest being 852 feet.

Now, only eleven years later Britain's Expeditionary Force arrived in France bringing with them their entire military air service - forty-eight aircraft. In the early phases of the war none of the combatant nations envisaged airplanes being enjoined in battle. Indeed it was not uncommon for pilots or their passenger-observers to wave greetings to enemy counterparts. The novelty of spotting mechanical objects in the skies elicited waves from the infantry below, both sides of the front line.

Within weeks of opening hostilities, however, a dramatic change in attitude came about.

Crucial information relayed from air observers to field commanders was resulting in the infliction of catastrophic horrors upon the parties observed. When the French Air Service reported sighting an illogical separation developing between the German 1st and 2nd Armies racing toward Paris the French Army reacted by driving a formidable wedge between the two enemy forces causing the German advance on

War in the Air

Paris to falter then collapse. Elsewhere the Allies suffered extensive casualties of men and materiel thought to have been safely ensconced in the rear. Apparently German field commanders were receiving reports from airborne observers that enabled them to accurately pinpoint remote targets. Heavy artillery then proceeded to pound Allied targets mercilessly. Both sides quickly developed a new appreciation for aviators.

Before 1914 ended, aircrew began to carry assorted firearms - mainly rifles, shotguns, machineguns. Machineguns were best for inflicting damage, but were heavy, awkward and difficult to aim. Aero engineers took up the challenge of developing new kinds of aircraft and weaponry, leaving pilots to concentrate on formulating tactics.

The German Air Service developed an *interrupter* for cowling-mounted machine guns. Interrupters synchronized a machinegun's firing rate with the rotation speed of the plane's propeller thus allowing bullets to pass between whirling prop blades without damaging them. German pilots now simply aimed their planes at a target and pulled the trigger. British planes were equipped with a swivel-mounted Lewis Gun; a drum-fed machinegun. The Lewis slid with relative ease along a track mounted atop the upper wing. However, for best results a pilot had to overtake his intended target from the rear, slip beneath the foe, position his plane, then open fire upward into the enemy's hull.

New generations of aircraft and weaponry were being designed, manufactured, and tested in great haste. Air crews were recruited largely from army volunteers. Preference was

Contempt for Danger

given to cavalrymen in the belief that good horsemanship produced good pilots. It also helped if candidates already knew how to drive a car or motorcycle. Learning to fly took anywhere from an hour to four days. New pilots having no previous machinegun experience were sent to an army base for training. Otherwise they were considered ready for the front. Tactical flying instruction was left up to squadron leaders at forward air bases. The mortality rate for new pilots in the early phases of the war was so high, aviators were considered lucky to survive their first two weeks at the front.

By the middle of 1916 a new order of battle had been introduced. Instead of reporting to army field commanders, most national air forces were re-organized and given their own chain of command. Evolving air forces became their own masters and while they continued to support ground forces, most no longer reported directly to army field commanders.

In 1917 the United States, Great Britain and Canada agreed to develop a universal pilot training program, selecting Camp Borden, Ontario and three airfields in the United States as their primary training centers. These training fields provided new recruits with instruction in flying, wireless operations, weapons, and photography. From April 1917 through December 1918 Camp Borden graduated 2,000 aircrew; 1,900 for service with the Royal Flying Corps, 100 for the United States Army.

Combatants were soon flying new fleets of aircraft. There were single-seat fighters for offense and others designed for defense. Two-seaters were used for bombing and

War in the Air

reconnaissance missions. Helium-filled balloons spotted for artillery. German dirigibles flew long range night missions to drop bombs on undefended cities. Many dirigibles cruised over England searching for targets of opportunity including London landmarks.

Massive air fleets brought large losses and the emergence of fighter aces. One of the earliest massive air battles occurred over Flanders in April of 1917. 176 of the 365 aircraft sent aloft by Britain's Royal Flying Corps (RFC) were destroyed by the enemy. In contrast, the German Air Service launched 100 aircraft yet lost only forty. German and Allied news media kept track of the names of pilots shooting down the greatest number of opposing aircraft.

As Canada had no air force many Canadian soldiers volunteered for service with Britain's RFC. Canadians flew all sorts of missions with the RFC in a wide variety of aircraft. Many became aces. Three Canadian aces received the Victoria Cross - Lieutenant Al McLeod from Stonewall, Manitoba, Captain Billy Bishop from Owen Sound, Ontario, and Lieutenant Colonel Will Barker of Dauphin, Manitoba.

Al McLeod was born in April, 1899 to parents of pioneer stock. His grandfather had emigrated from Scotland, settled in the west and became an employee of the Hudson's Bay Company. Al's father was a medical doctor. His mother was a Selkirk settler before Manitoba became a province. On his eighteenth birthday, the earliest age he was permitted to do so, Al McLeod enlisted in the cadet wing of the Royal Flying Corps in Toronto. He soloed after seven weeks training at Long

Contempt for Danger

Branch, Ontario and was then sent to Camp Borden to complete his instruction. By late November of 1917 young Al McLeod was flying over France as an Armstrong-Whitney bomber pilot with Number 2 Squadron. His missions involved bombing, artillery spotting and photographic reconnaissance.

Lieutenant McLeod proved to be an excellent pilot. It was most unusual for bomber pilots to shoot down enemy aircraft but McLeod was the exception. He enabled his gunner to get a clear shot by maneuvering his bomber close to German marauders. On other occasions he was able to fire his own forward-aimed machineguns. There were times when McLeod flew three successive bombing missions a night then went up again next morning to conduct photo reconnaissance. On March 21, 1918 Lieutenant McLeod and his gunner/observer Lieutenant A.W. Hammond had just destroyed an enemy triplane over Albert, France when they were set upon by eight German attackers. The Germans swarmed around them, firing from every direction. Nevertheless McLeod and Hammond shot down two more triplanes. McLeod and Hammond were seriously wounded when machinegun bullets suddenly riddled their fuselage from below and set their gas tank on fire. McLeod dove toward the ground, side-slipping to keep the flames from licking at Hammond. They crash-landed in no-man's land, their plane burning fiercely. Eight heavy bombs were still aboard. Hammond, who had been wounded six times, was helpless. Although McLeod had five wounds, he was able to drag Hammond out and away from the blazing aircraft. McLeod suffered his sixth wound when bombs and

War in the Air

ammunition aboard their plane began to explode. Mustering a supreme effort McLeod picked up Hammond and toted him to the relative safety of an Allied forward position before collapsing from exhaustion. Within days McCleod was transported to a London hospital where he began a lengthy and painful recovery; for months hovering between life and death.

Second Lieutenant Alan McCleod was the youngest Canadian ever to receive a Victoria Cross. Alan's doctor father had been with him in England for several weeks. Both attended Alan's VC investiture at Buckingham Palace on September 4, 1918. A few days later the McCleods sailed for Canada. When their train arrived in Winnipeg Alan McCleod was feted to a festive welcome by the city. Once back home in Stonewall, Alan McLeod's health began to improve steadily. However, he contracted a strain of virulent influenza. Alan Arnett McLeod died in a Winnipeg hospital November 6, 1918. He was only nineteen years of age.

More than 35,000 Canadians died that year and next from a strain of Spanish Flu sweeping North America. Risk of catching the highly contagious killer-flu was so great the 1919 Stanley Cup hockey playoffs were cancelled. Many blamed the influenza epidemic on troops returning from Europe where the flu was also raging.

16
Bishop & Barker

Born in Owen Sound, Ontario in 1894 *William Avery Bishop* was a student at Royal Military College in Kingston when war broke out. At twenty years of age he immediately volunteered for service with the Canadian Expeditionary Force. Commissioned as a cavalry lieutenant, young Bishop's unit shipped overseas without him because at the time he was recovering from a bout of pneumonia. When he eventually arrived in Britain, Bishop transferred to the RFC. For five months Billy flew as an observer before being trained as a pilot. In early 1917 Billy Bishop was sent to Arras, France. Within two months Bishop downed seventeen enemy aircraft and had become his squadron's leading ace. As flight commander of the *Flying Foxes,* RFC 60 Squadron, Bishop received a *Distinguished Flying Cross* after shooting down twenty-five enemy aircraft in twelve days.

Captain Bishop was only twenty-three when he was awarded the Victoria Cross for actions on June 2, 1917. It happened when he was patrolling alone over Cambrai, France and noticed a flight of four aircraft on a German base warming up for take-off. One plane actually lifted from the ground but was quickly downed by Bishop who then turned to the next plane racing down the runway. His machinegun fire unnerved the German pilot causing him to swerve and crash into a tree.

Bishop & Barker

In the time it took Bishop to circle the field the last two aircraft were airborne. Bishop emptied his Lewis Gun into one of the planes causing it to crash. As Bishop was loading a fresh ammunition drum the fourth flier got onto his tail. Bishop deftly eluded his pursuer then emptied his machine-gun at the foe. The German scooted away and Bishop flew home.

By war's end Billy Bishop had downed 72 enemy aircraft, a record only slightly exceeded by the eighty kills credited to Germany's most famous ace Manfred von Richthofen - *the Red Baron*. Captain Bishop, the Allies highest scoring ace, was also awarded the Military Cross and French Croix de Guerre as well as the French Legion d'Honneur.

William George Barker was born in Dauphin, Manitoba in 1894. Just before the outbreak of war his family moved to Winnipeg. In December 1914 Will Barker enlisted in the 1st Canadian Mounted Rifles. His unit shipped to England in the summer of 1915. Although a trained cavalryman, Barker was sent to France as a machinegunner and fought in the Second Battle of Ypres. In the summer of 1915 Will Barker was accepted in the RFC. Following six days of training he was sent to Bertangles, France to join Number 9 Squadron as an observer/gunner. During the Battle of the Somme in the summer of 1916 2nd Lieutenant Barker shot down two enemy planes. On a subsequent flight he was wounded in the thigh. Lieutenant Barker was awarded his first decoration, the Military Cross, a few weeks after returning to duty for taking critical reconnaissance photos while under almost constant attack by enemy fighters. Early in 1917 Barker completed pilot

Contempt for Danger

training in Narborough, England. Soon after returning to France he was promoted to captain and made a flight commander. In August Captain Barker suffered a head wound and passed out from loss of blood yet recovered sufficiently to land his plane safely. In October he was assigned to fly a Sopwith Camel with 28th Fighter Squadron. His Camel was armed with twin Vickers machineguns and, at times, four twenty pound bombs.

Within a few weeks Barker had become an ace. It came about as their flight of six Camels was strafing German troops on the ground when they were attacked by a flight of German Albatross fighters who quickly shot down two of the Camels. An Albatross got on Barker's tail and riddled his plane from cockpit to tail. Barker made a very tight turn then pulled up into a loop. Coming down he came in behind the Albatross that had been pursuing him. A short burst downed the enemy - Barker's fifth kill. When another Albatross got behind him, Barker repeated his loop maneuver and brought down his sixth enemy plane. He got his seventh two days later.

By late 1917 the Italian Army was facing collapse after having failed to stem a massive Austro/Hungarian offensive. Italy's allies, Britain and France, each dispatched four squadrons to bolster Italian air defenses. Will Barker was one of the few Canadians to serve in Italy during the Great War. Following an exciting and productive year in Italy, Barker was posted back to the Western Front.

Major Barker earned his Victoria Cross on October 27, 1918 while flying a Sopwith Snipe over Foret de Mormal, France. His attack on a two-seater enemy aircraft caused it to explode in the air. Barker was in turn attacked by a formation of German Fokker fighters. Bullets hit him in both thighs, a third shattered his elbow. Fading in and out of consciousness, Barker miraculously mustered a counterattack and shot down three Fokkers. Bleeding profusely from his wounds and in intense pain, Major Will Barker struggled to keep his bullet riddled Snipe in the air, eventually crash-landing it on the British side. He was pulled from the aircraft unconscious, yet alive.

Barker suffered through a lengthy recovery. In January he was moved to England. His thighs never quite healed, and he was left partially disabled and suffering from intermittent pain. In the spring of 1919, with one arm in a sling and using a cane, newly promoted Lieutenant Colonel Will Barker had the honor of taking Britain's Prince of Wales on a half hour flight over London in a new two-seater Sopwith Dove.

Will Barker was credited with destroying fifty enemy aircraft during the war. Apart from his Victoria Cross, Lieutenant Colonel Barker earned a Distinguished Service Order and bar, Military Cross and two bars, France's Croix de Guerre, and Italy's Valore Militare.

After returning to Canada Billy Bishop teamed up with Will Barker to form the Bishop & Barker Company, a commercial air service flying between Toronto's Island Airport and the Ontario resort community of Muskoka. With only limited demand for their service the business was soon wound up. The air aces then contracted with the Canadian National Exhibition to perform aerobatic stunts over the grandstand at Toronto's Exhibition

Contempt for Danger

Park. With thoughts of adding a touch of excitement to their aerial display, Bishop and Barker decided at the last moment to buzz the stands. The startled crowd panicked and stampeded toward the exits. Barker and Bishop were fired and soon went their separate way.

Will Barker joined Canada's new air force in its formative years, then tried his hand at tobacco farming near Simcoe, Ontario. In 1929, after recovering from a severe bout of pneumonia, Barker quit farming to accept the presidency of Montreal based Fairchild Aviation. Three months later, while demonstrating a new Fairchild two-seater aircraft for the War Office at Ottawa's Rockliffe Airport, Will Barker was killed when his plane failed to pull out of a dive. William George Barker, one of Canada's most decorated war heroes, died March 12, 1930 at age thirty-six.

Billy Bishop worked a number of years in the oil industry. In 1938 he was invited to head an advisory committee responsible for rapidly expanding Canada's fledgling air force. Air Marshal William Avery Bishop retired in 1944. He died twelve years later, at age sixty-two.

In December 1917 downtown Halifax, Nova Scotia was obliterated by a horrendous explosion triggered by the collision of the Norwegian ship Iwo with the French munitions ship *Mont Blanc* in Halifax harbor. The detonation was heard fifty miles away. The blast leveled the city, killing close to two thousand people and injuring another nine thousand.

17
Spring 1918

Rain and snow brought fighting to a virtual halt along the entire Western Front in the winter of 1917 - 1918. During this hiatus no great offenses were initiated on land or in the air. Endless tracts of mud had frozen rock solid. Occasionally an artillery shell would deflect off the ground, fail to explode, only to skitter crazily across frozen terrain in unpredictable directions. In winter the infantry mainly battled the cold, trench-foot, and such illnesses as bronchitis, influenza and pneumonia. Gradually the days became longer and thankfully warmer. The milder weather also motivated the Germans to make an all out, do-or-die effort.

The *Ludendorf Offensive* struck on the first day of spring 1918 along a sixty mile front. Its surprise and force initially overwhelmed Allied defenses. British forces fell back toward the coast. The French army drew a tight defensive cordon around Paris. The American Expeditionary Force braced for its first major battle.

The Germans advanced forty miles within two weeks before resistance stiffened. During that time the British suffered 60,000 casualties. In the U.S. sector of the front the United States Marines 6th Regiment halted the German onslaught at Chateau Thierry.

Contempt for Danger

On March 21, 1918 thirty-four year old Irish/Canadian *Edmund de Wind* was serving as a second lieutenant with the British Army's 15th Battalion, Royal Irish Rifle Regiment. For the past seven hours Lieutenant de Wind had defended an important position near Groagie, France while all around him his platoon was being slowly decimated. Although suffering from two wounds, de Wind continued to hold the position while awaiting relief. Twice under heavy fire, he and two of his non-commissioned officers climbed from their trench to get better shots at the advancing Germans, repelling attack after attack. By the time the relief unit broke through, Lieutenant de Wind lay mortally wounded. His Victoria Cross was awarded posthumously.

George McKean was a platoon leader with 14th Battalion, Royal Montreal Regiment. On the night of April 27th the lieutenant's unit was pinned down by intense enemy fire near Gavrelle, France. They were stalled before a safety block built into the communications trench. Leaping over the safety block Lieutenant McKean landed on top of an enemy soldier. McKean was immediately attacked by a second German wielding a rifle with fixed bayonet. McKean shot them both. Lieutenant McKean captured the position and sent for more hand-grenades. In the meantime he fiercely defended the position on his own. He again leaped from the trench and ran to a second trench-block where he killed two more Germans and captured four others. Several enemy soldiers ducked into a dug-out which McKean promptly blew-up. Twenty-nine year old Lieutenant George Burdon McKean had earned his Victoria

86

Spring 1918

Cross and was later promoted to captain. Mount McKean in Jasper National Park, Alberta is named in his honor.

The sole Canadian in the naval service to receive a Victoria Cross was **Roland Bourke**. Thirty-two year old Bourke was a lieutenant in the Royal Navy in command of Motor Torpedo Boat 216. The HMS Vindictive had just been sunk in the harbor of Ostend, Belgium on the night of May 9, 1918. All the crew had reportedly been taken off the sinking vessel. Lieutenant Bourke was under constant enemy fire when he took MTB 216 into the harbor to ensure that everyone had indeed gotten away. After searching the water without success, he began to withdraw from the harbor when faint cries for help were heard. Turning back, MTB 216 rescued an officer and two seamen clinging to an overturned lifeboat. 216, by this time, had sustained fifty-five enemy hits including one from a six inch shell that killed two of her crew and badly damaged the boat. Bourke maneuvered his crippled boat safely beyond the harbor entrance where it was taken under tow by another Royal Navy craft. In addition to his Victoria Cross, Roland Richard Louis Bourke subsequently earned a Distinguished Service Order. Later he attained the rank of lieutenant commander. Roland Bourke eventually retired to Victoria, British Columbia.

Another Canadian to earn the Victoria Cross while serving under British command was **Bob Cruickshank**. He was a private with 14th Battalion, London Scottish Regiment, British Army. The London Scottish was engaged in battle east of Jordan, Palestine. On May 1st 1918 Private Cruickshank's platoon was cut off and forced to take cover at the bottom of a

Contempt for Danger

desert ravine. The platoon was in dire straights. The sole remaining officer and most of the men had been wounded. Bob Cruickshank volunteered to carry a message to company headquarters. Private Cruickshank plodded up the sandy slope but as he crested the top he fell wounded. Cruickshank arose and had just begun to move forward again when he was hit a second time. He slithered back down the dune. After getting his wounds dressed he made a third attempt to get through. He was wounded a third time and now could scarcely move. Suffering all day long Bob Cruickshank lay dangerously exposed to his enemies who continued to take random pot shots at him, wounding him several more times. The lost platoon was eventually rescued. Private Robert Edward Cruickshank was awarded the Victoria Cross for exceptional bravery. He remained in the army, later earned his commission and rose to the rank of major.

Back home the Canadian government extended the right to women to vote in federal elections. However, the new law failed to include Native peoples, or persons of Chinese or Japanese origin. During the summer Canadian Prime Minister Robert Borden sailed to Britain to reinforce Canada's plea for a say in strategic military decisions. Canada now had 500,000 troops in Europe but no voice in military strategy. London dismissed the Canadian complaint, arguing that Canada was attempting to act as an ally rather than a dutiful family member.

18
Amiens, France

In May of 1918 Canada's Expeditionary Force was withdrawn from the line to undergo special training for the upcoming battle of Amiens. Amiens was on the River Somme lying between Abbeville on the west and Peronne, France. The Amiens sector was the most southern position the Canadian Expeditionary Force was to serve. The CEF was given training as shock troops and placed in the vanguard of the great battle fought August 8 - 11, 1918.

As German intelligence was aware of the British practice of using Canadians as shock troops, the Canucks were inserted into the line with great secrecy. Australian troops anchored the Canadians left flank, French troops held the right. British tanks would reinforce the Canadian push. The assault caught the Germans by surprise, moving with such velocity that within three days the Canucks had penetrated two miles beyond the initial German defense line.

Within one hundred days the war would be over. Yet the troops had no way of knowing this. The German Army put up a vigorous defense whenever provoked. Canadians were destined to fight almost continuously until war's end.

Winnipegger *Jimmy Tait* was attached to 18th Battalion, Manitoba Regiment. Although most units had moved forward,

Contempt for Danger

18th Battalion was held in check by intense enemy machinegun fire. Under a hail of bullets Lieutenant Tait advanced with his infantry company. When they bogged down, Jim Tait continued alone to the closest machinegun. When he killed the German gunner his company rushed to him and together they captured twelve machineguns plus twenty Germans. Later they were subjected to heavy artillery fire followed by an enemy counterattack. The bravery of thirty-two year old James Edward Tate served as an inspiration to his men long after he fell fatally wounded. His Victoria Cross was awarded posthumously. Earlier he had received a Military Cross. Lieutenant James Tate is buried near Albert, France.

On August 8, 1918 two members of 13th Battalion, Quebec Regiment - *the Royal Highlanders* - each earned a Victoria Cross: Private Johnnie Croak and Corporal Herman Good.

Born in 1892, **Johnnie Croak** was only fourteen when he quit school to work in the mines to help support his family. Five years later the Maritimer moved out west to work in the wheat fields. Johnnie joined the army and fought in major battles at the Somme, Vimy Ridge, Arras, Hill 70, Passchendaele and Amiens. On August 8, 1918 twenty-six year old Private John Croak had become separated from his section when he stumbled across a German machinegun post. Croak immobilized the nest by lobbing a hand-grenade into it. He quickly captured the gun and took its crew prisoner. Private Croak was severely wounded while leading the captives back to his platoon. Refusing an offer to be taken to a rear dressing station, he elected to move forward with his platoon. His unit

Amiens, France

soon came face to face with several German machineguns. Instinctively Johnnie Croak raced forward; his platoon right behind him. The Canadians leapt into a German trench and, with fixed-bayonets, dispatched the enemy. Those not killed quickly surrendered. Unfortunately John Bernard Croak was fatally wounded in the melee. His Victoria Cross was awarded posthumously.

Corporal Herman Good's company was held up by the staccato of three enemy machineguns. The corporal dashed forward alone. Using his rifle with fixed-bayonet, and hand-grenades Corporal Good killed several Germans and took the remainder prisoner. He had captured a triple machinegun post. Later the thirty year old corporal came upon a German artillery battery shelling the Canadian line. Without hesitation he took three men from his section and charged the gun emplacements, capturing all three German artillery pieces and their crews.

Two men from 22nd Battalion, Canadien Francais Regiment earned the Victoria Cross the summer of 1918. Joe Kaeble earned his Victoria Cross for actions on June 8, and Jean Brillant exactly two months later on August 8th.

While in charge of a machinegun section at Neuville-Vitasse twenty-five year old *Corporal Joseph Kaeble* came under heavy enemy attack. All but one of his crew fell wounded. As soon as the enemy artillery barrage lifted about fifty German grenadiers charged their post. Corporal Kaeble leapt atop the parapet with his Lewis gun and, firing from the hip, pumped one magazine drum after another into the

Contempt for Danger

advancing enemy. Although hit several times Corporal Kaeble continued to fire from his exposed position. The enemy advance faltered. The Germans were beginning to retreat when Kaeble fell mortally wounded. Joseph Kaeble was awarded his Victoria Cross posthumously and is buried near Arras, France.

Lieutenant Jean Brillant was wounded while capturing an enemy machinegun that had pinned down his company. In order to retain command Brillant refused evacuation to the rear, instead, opting to have his wound hastily dressed. When another machinegun slowed their advance Lieutenant Brillant took two of his platoons and rushed the enemy post. He was wounded a second time while completing the capture of 150 Germans and a dozen machineguns. Again he settled for a battlefield dressing and pressed on. That afternoon he was wounded a third time while leading a rush to knock out a German field gun. He fell unconscious and died the following day. He was twenty-eight. In addition to his Victoria Cross, Jean Brillant had recently been awarded the Military Cross. He is buried at Fouilloy, ten miles east of Amiens.

Just about the time Lieutenant Brillant was earning his medal of valor *Corporal Harry Miner* of 58th Battalion, 2nd Central Ontario Regiment single-handedly rushed a German machinegun. He killed the entire crew and turned the gun on the enemy. Later, with two other Canadian infantrymen, he attacked a second machinegun post, knocking it out of action. Still later, Harry Miner charged a third enemy post. When he bayoneted two Germans the others fled. He was mortally wounded in the fray. Harry Garnet Bedford Miner died at

Amiens, France

twenty-seven years of age. He was awarded the Victoria Cross as well as the French Croix de Guerre posthumously.

The following day, August 9, 1918 four Canadian soldiers earned a Victoria Cross - Corporal Al Brereton, Corporal Fred Coppins, Private Thomas Dinesen, and Sergeant Raphael Zengel.

Corporal Al Brereton was advancing across open ground when German machineguns opened fire on his exposed platoon. He realized that unless something was done immediately, they would be annihilated. So, twenty-five year old Corporal Brereton made a beeline toward the closest machinegun. He shot the gunner and bayoneted a second German. Nine other Germans surrendered to Brereton. The corporal's brave action inspired the rest of his platoon to rush forward and capture five other machinegun posts. Alexander Picton Brereton later attained the rank of Company Quartermaster.

Similar to Al Brereton's experience, *Corporal Fred Coppins* found himself pinned down in the open by several enemy machineguns. His platoon could neither advance nor fall back. Coppins collected four men and rushed straight toward the nearest gun. Coppins fell wounded; the other four were shot dead. Despite his wound Frederick George Coppins arose and crawled to the enemy post where he killed four Germans and took four more prisoner. Inspired by his action, the rest of his platoon quickly advanced to the captured machinegun then resumed the advance on their initial objective.

Thomas Dinesen came from Rungsted, Denmark where he was born in 1892. When war broke out young Dinesen tried to

Contempt for Danger

enlist in the British, French and American armies. All declined his offer. The persistent young man was finally accepted as a private with 42nd Battalion, Quebec Regiment (the Royal Highlanders). Dinesen displayed conspicuous bravery on August 2, 1918 during ten hours of hand-to-hand fighting near Parvillers, France which resulted in the capture of a mile of strongly defended enemy trenches. Twenty-six year old Private Dinesen repeatedly led his platoon in bayonet rushes. Using his bayonet and grenades Dinesen killed twelve German grenadiers while putting several hostile guns out of action. His Victoria Cross citation notes Dinesen's *sustained valor inspired his comrades at a very critical stage of the action.* Thomas Dinesen also earned a Croix de Guerre. He later attained the rank of lieutenant.

Born in Faribault, Minnesota November 11, 1894 **Raphael Louis Zengel** immigrated to Canada to sign up with 5th Battalion, Saskatchewan Regiment. Sergeant Zengel was leading his platoon east of Warvillers, France on August 9, 1918 when they encountered a German machinegun. Sergeant Zengel rushed forward on his own to the gun emplacement and killed the officer in charge and the gunner. The rest of the German gun crew fled. Later that day Zengel was knocked unconscious by an exploding enemy shell. When he came to he directed harassing fire against the enemy. In part his Victoria Cross citation reads: *His utter disregard for personal safety and the confidence he inspired in all ranks greatly assisted in the successful outcome of the attack.* Sergeant Zengel had earlier been awarded the Military Medal. Raphael Zengel died in 1977 while in

Amiens, France

British Columbia and is interred at Rocky Mountain, Alberta. Mount Zengel in Jasper National Park is named in his honor.

Born in Ealing, England in 1890 Sergeant **Robert Spall** of the Princess Patricia Canadian Light Infantry regiment deliberately sacrificed his life in order to extricate his platoon from a most difficult situation. It happened the night of August 12, 1918. Cut-off from the rest of their company, Sergeant Spall's platoon became the focus of a strong German counterattack. Spall grabbed a Lewis gun, climbed onto the parapet and fired directly into the advancing enemy, inflicting many casualties. Dropping back into the trench he directed his men to a relatively safe position three hundred feet away, then picked up his Lewis gun, climbed back atop the parapet and opened fire. His platoon was able to scramble to safety but Robert Spall fell mortally wounded. His Victoria Cross was awarded posthumously.

Charlie Rutherford was born in 1892 and grew up on a farm near Colborne, Ontario. Charlie joined the army in 1916 at age twenty-four. He shipped overseas with 5th Canadian Mounted Rifles Battalion, Quebec Regiment. The 5th fought at Ypres before shifting to the Somme front where Charlie was wounded. Charlie Rutherford was discharged from a military hospital in England in time to fight at Vimy Ridge. He was wounded again and didn't return to the front until August of 1917. Charlie was awarded the Military Medal for his actions as a sergeant in the battle for Passchendaele. After completing officer training in England, Charlie Rutherford was elevated to second lieutenant. As a platoon commander in August 1918

Contempt for Danger

Lieutenant Rutherford earned a Military Cross. On August 26th Lieutenant Charles Rutherford was leading a raiding party near Monchy, France when he realized he had gotten too far ahead of his men. He also observed a strong enemy force assembling before a pillbox. Twenty-six year old Lieutenant Rutherford pulled off a fantastic bluff by convincing the enemy they were surrounded. Forty-five Germans including two officers surrendered and gave up their two heavy machineguns. Lieutenant Rutherford later led a Lewis gun detachment in an attack against another German machinegun post, capturing 35 Germans as well as their machineguns. Following the war Charlie married Helen Haig and together they raised a son and three daughters. Charlie pursued a varied career: dairy farmer, Sergeant-at-Arms for the Ontario Legislature, drygoods merchant, and postmaster of Colborne. He even found time to serve four years with the Canadian army during World War II, departing with the rank of captain. He retired in 1979. Prior to his death on June 11, 1989 Charlie Rutherford held the distinction of being the last surviving Canadian Victoria Cross recipient of the Great War.

The day after Lieutenant Rutherford tricked the Germans into surrendering, another battalion from Quebec Regiment - the 24th commanded by *Lieutenant Colonel Bill Clark-Kennedy* - suffered heavy casualties. An entire Canadian brigade was halted by intense German fire along the Fresnes-Rouvroy line near Amiens. Lieutenant Colonel Clark-Kennedy mustered his men and led them forward, collecting stragglers along the way. He also encouraged

Amiens, France

neighboring battalions on his flanks to move ahead with him in unison. The entire brigade benefited from Clark-Kennedy's counterattack by shifting forward. The next day, August 28th, Clark-Kennedy was severely wounded. Despite extreme pain and weakness from loss of blood, the 24th's commander refused to be evacuated until reaching a position from which the advance could be resumed. In addition to his Victoria Cross, thirty-nine year old William Hew Clark-Kennedy was awarded France's Croix de Guerre.

Canada's victory at Amiens was one of the great triumphs of the war. Although the Allies sustained about forty thousand casualties, the Germans lost twice the Allies' rate including 30,000 taken prisoner. Ahead lay the *Hindenburg Line* - a twenty mile wide complex of trenches, barbed wire and heavily defended fortifications.

19
The Canadian Cavalry Brigade

Winnie delighted many young fans at England's London Zoo. *Captain Harry Colborn* purchased the black bear in Winnipeg for $20 upon learning a hunter had shot the cub's mother. Colborn named his bear Winnipeg - Winnie for short - after his hometown. When Captain Colborn shipped overseas he took Winnie along. The bear cub slept beneath his bunk. When his outfit was ordered to the front, Captain Colborn donated Winnie to the London Zoo. Colborn's bear was immortalized by famous English author A. A. Milne in his children's series classic *Winnie the Pooh.*

The origin of the 34th Fort Garry Horse can be traced to Winnipeg where Lieutenant Colonel R. W. Paterson trained his new cavalry regiment as a *sword and rifle* outfit. The 34th was sent to Valcartier, Quebec to be combined with other western Canadian cavalry units to create the 6th Fort Garry Horse Regiment. The 6th's cap badge featured a replica of Winnipeg's Fort Garry gate atop a maple leaf overlaid with a scroll reading *6 Fort Garry Horse.* At Valcartier the new regiment learned astonishing news. They were told that modern warfare had rendered cavalry redundant owing to the profusion of barbed wire, machineguns and rapid fire artillery. They were ordered to relinquish their horses. The horseless 6th Fort Garry Horse

The Canadian Cavalry Brigade

regiment shipped overseas with orders to undertake infantry training at Salisbury Plain in southern England.

After living outdoors for several months, training on cold wind-swept plains, good news arrived. Fresh horses were to be issued. A Canadian Cavalry Brigade was being formed comprising four regiments of Canadian cavalry plus one British regiment. The brigade landed in France with four of its five regiments: the Canadian Dragoons, Lord Strathcona Horse, Canadian Horse Artillery and Britain's 2nd King Edward Regiment. The 6th Fort Garry Horse regiment was to remain in England as a training and replacement depot for the battle units.

The *Royal Canadian Dragoons* regiment was formed in 1883 and won its first battle honors helping to quell the Riel Rebellion in 1885. In the Boer War three of the regiment's troopers were awarded the Victoria Cross for actions in the battle of Leliefontien November 7, 1900. The *Lord Strathcona Horse* regiment was, of course, Lieutenant Colonel Sam Steele's old outfit. The regiment earned its first battle honors during in the Boer War. The *Royal Canadian Horse Artillery Regiment* came from Kingston, Ontario. With their horses harnessed to 13 pounder guns, the Royal Canadian Horse was the mobile artillery of the new Canadian Cavalry Brigade.

Dreams of long rides and dashing charges - made romantically popular in the days of the Riel Rebellion and Boer War - quickly dissolved. It was patently obvious from the extensive trench systems of the Western Front, to say nothing of its mud, the European battlefield was not conducive to

Contempt for Danger

classical cavalry maneuvers. Instead, cavalry troopers were often deployed as infantry, road builders, or transporters of supplies, ammunition and other war materiel.

Early in 1916 the 6th Fort Garry Horse was ordered to France to replace Britain's King Edward Regiment. The Canadian Cavalry Brigade was now totally Canadian. Canada's cavalry fought many battles and participated in several significant assaults such as the Somme, Amiens, Arras, Cambrai and Hill 70. Many troopers shared extraordinary experiences. Three were awarded the Victoria Cross: Lieutenant Fred Harvey, Lieutenant Harcus Strachan, and Lieutenant Gordon Flowerdew.

Fred Harvey was born in Athboy, Ireland in 1888. He immigrated to Canada in 1908 where he initially took work as a surveyor in northern Alberta. Three years later Fred settled in Fort MacLeod. With the advent of war Fred Harvey enlisted in the Canadian Mounted Rifles, but shipped overseas as a lieutenant with the Lord Strathcona Horse. On March 27, 1917 the regiment was attacking a village near Guyencourt, France when German grenadiers ran toward a trench in front of the village. The village was wreathed in barbed wire. An enemy machinegun opened fire. Rapid enemy fire at such close range caused heavy casualties amongst the advancing Strathconas. Troop commander Lieutenant Harvey swung from his saddle and raced to the German trench. Leaping over the barbed wire entanglement, Harvey shot the gunners and captured the enemy machinegun. Frederick Harvey was awarded the Victoria Cross for his courageous actions. In addition to his VC,

The Canadian Cavalry Brigade

Fred Harvey was also a recipient of the Military Cross and French Croix de Guerre. Harvey was a physical education instructor at Royal Military College in Kingston for several years following the war. In 1938 he was promoted to lieutenant colonel and given command of the army's Currie Barracks in Calgary. From 1940 - 1946 Brigadier General Fred Harvey commanded 13th Alberta Military District. Throughout his active life he remained an avid equestrian, taking part in many horse shows. Frederick Maurice Watson Harvey died in 1980 at age 92. Mount Harvey in Jasper National Park is named in his honor.

On November 20th 1917 *Lieutenant Harcus Strachan*, a thirty-three year old Scottish/Canadian from Winnipeg, Manitoba, assumed command of a squadron of the Fort Garry Horse after its regimental commander, Captain Campbell, was shot off his horse. Drawing his saber, Lieutenant Strachan led the squadron at full gallop toward a line of machineguns defending a German artillery battery. Leaping across the enemy lines with saber flashing, Lieutenant Strachan slashed and skewered seven enemy gunners. The battery was silenced. Unfortunately only 43 cavalrymen, out of the squadron's original 130, survived. Worse, they were now isolated behind German lines. When night fell, Lieutenant Strachan ordered his men to stampede their horses as a diversionary tactic. The lieutenant then led his men safely back to the Canadian lines, bringing with them all of their wounded plus fifteen German prisoners. Harcus Strachan received the Victoria Cross for his display of valor that day. He is also a recipient of the Military

101

Cross. During the Second World War Harcus Strachan, by then a lieutenant colonel, commanded 1st Battalion, Edmonton Fusiliers.

When the Germans launched their Ludendorf Offensive in March 1918 the Canadian Cavalry Brigade fought many mounted and dismounted rear guard actions to relieve hard pressed infantry units. On March 30th the entire Canadian Cavalry Brigade attacked the Germans at Bois de Moreuil.

Gordon Flowerdew was born in Billingsford, Norfolk County England in 1885. At 18 he immigrated to Canada, settling initially in Duck Lake Saskatchewan before moving on to Wallachin, British Columbia. When war broke out Gordon enlisted in the 31st British Columbia Horse Battalion, later transferring to the Lord Strathcona Horse Regiment. On March 30, 1918 Lieutenant Flowerdew led his cavalry squadron on a special mission near Moreuil Woods. As they neared their objective the troopers' way was blocked by two German defense lines. Upwards of sixty Germans were estimated to be in the first trench and an equal number in the second trench about 200 yards further away. Both trench lines had positioned machineguns on each flank and in the center. Lieutenant Flowerdew ordered Lieutenant Harvey's troop to dismount and engage the enemy. With sabers raised, Lieutenant Flowerdew led his remaining three cavalry units at full gallop. They slashed the German defenders as they tore through the line. Wheeling about, the cavalry squadron raised their sabers again and came full tilt at the Germans from the rear. The enemy fled in panic. Flowerdew's daring squadron achieved

102

The Canadian Cavalry Brigade

it's objective but at significant cost. Seventy percent of Flowerdew's cavalry was wiped out. Gordon Flowerdew, the squadron commander was seriously wounded in both thighs and died within hours. His Victoria Cross was awarded posthumously. Gordon Muriel Flowerdew is buried near Amiens.

The Canadian Cavalry Brigade fought its final action of the war at Gattigny Wood in October of 1918.

20
Hindenburg Line

Canada's Expeditionary Force was ordered to smash through the Hindenburg defenses on the Drocourt-Queant (DQ) Line near Arras. Canadian forces attacked on August 26, completing their mission on September 2, 1918.

Seven brave Canadians earned a Victoria Cross during the successful penetration of the DQ Line: Private Claude Nunney, Sergeant Art Knight, Lieutenant Colonel Cyrus Peck, Lance Corporal William Metcalf, Captain Bellendem Hutcheson, Private Johnnie Young and Private Walter Rayfield.

Born in England in 1891 *Claude Nunney* was orphaned at an early age. Claude was a teenager when brought to Canada in 1905 as a ward of the government and settled in North Lancaster, Ontario. Claude joined the army in 1913 at age twenty-two and shipped overseas with 38th Battalion, Eastern Ontario Regiment. In early September of 1918 the regiment was defending itself against a counterattack on the DQ Line when Private Claude Nunney, acting on his own initiative, eased his way through the barrage to the forward perimeter of the Canadian line. Nunney crept from outpost to outpost offering words of encouragement to men in remote dug-outs. The enemy counterattack was repulsed. The next day Nunney's company joined a major assault that broke through the DQ Line. While advancing toward their objective Private Nunney

104

Hindenburg Line

again displayed the highest degree of valor until severely wounded. His wounds proved fatal, and his Victoria Cross was awarded posthumously. In addition to his VC, Claude Joseph Patrick Nunney was also the recipient of a Distinguished Conduct Medal and the Military Medal.

Art Knight, a sergeant with 10th Battalion Alberta Regiment, was leading a bombing mission near Cagnicourt on September 2nd when enemy fire brought them to a halt. Sergeant Knight went on alone, bayoneting enemy machinegunners and trench mortar crews. Knight returned to snatch up a Lewis gun to fire at the retreating enemy. As the Canadians pursued the fleeing Germans, Sergeant Knight noticed a platoon of enemy grenadiers duck into a tunnel. Knight approached the tunnel alone and succeeded in killing a German officer plus two grenadiers; he took twenty Germans prisoner. Later in the day thirty-two year old Arthur George Knight was fatally wounded while routing-out another enemy unit. In addition to his Victoria Cross, Sergeant Knight was awarded the French Croix de Guerre.

Lieutenant Colonel Cyrus Peck commanded 16th Battalion, Manitoba Regiment. His troops were pinned down by enemy machinegun fire soon after they had achieved their first objective of the day. Ignoring the heavy fire Lieutenant Colonel Peck made his own personal reconnaissance of the situation. Upon his return he re-organized his battalion then sent them forward. Under intense artillery and machinegun fire Peck strode into the open, intercepted a passing squadron of Allied tanks and re-directed them toward the German machinegun

Contempt for Danger

posts. His battalion fell in behind the tanks as they moved toward their objective. That day forty-seven year old Cyrus Wesley Peck earned a Victoria Cross to wear alongside his Distinguished Service Order medal.

Billy Metcalf was born in 1894 in Walsh County, Maine. In the summer of 1914, at age 20, Billy crossed the international boundary without advising his mother of his intentions and joined the Canadian Army at Fredericton, New Brunswick. Two months later Private *William Metcalf* shipped overseas with 12th Battalion. Alerted to where she might locate her son, Billy's mother arranged for the United States Ambassador to Britain to meet her son's troop ship when it arrived in England. The Ambassador's intervention was to no avail. On his enlistment papers twenty year old Billy Metcalf reported his age as twenty-nine. This variance plus Billy's insistence he was raised on a farm in St. David Ridge, New Brunswick rather than Waite, Maine enabled him to deceive the authorities. In May of 1915 Metcalfe transferred to Lieutenant Colonel Cyrus Peck's 16th Battalion, Manitoba Regiment and shipped to France. At the front Billy Metcalfe was wounded twice, and earned the Military Medal for gallantry. He earned his Victoria Cross on September 2, 1918 when the 16th's right flank was held up at Arras. Metcalf rushed forward under intense machinegun fire to intercept a passing Allied tank. Using a signal flag to point directions, Corporal Metcalf proceeded in front of the tank while directing it along a trench. Under a hail of bullets and shells they inflicted heavy casualties on the enemy as they overran a German machinegun nest. Wounded

106

Hindenburg Line

in the fray, Metcalf continued to advance until ordered into a shell hole to have his wounds dressed. After the war the American born Canadian Army hero returned to Maine where he pursued a career as an auto mechanic. William Metcalf died in 1968 at age seventy-five (his real age).

Yet another gallant American to serve with Canada's armed forces was Bell Hutcheson. *Bellenden Seymour Hutcheson* was born in Illinois in 1883 and graduated with a medical degree from Northwestern University. Bell's Scottish grandfather had immigrated to the United States in the 1840s and served as an officer with a New York regiment during the Civil War. In 1915, at age 32, Bell Hutcheson crossed into Canada and enlisted with the Army Medical Corps. He was attached to 75th Battalion, 1st Central Ontario Regiment - the *Toronto Scottish*. He earned his Military Cross serving with the Toronto Scottish on August 8, 1918. 75th Battalion was jumping-off from a village eighty miles north of Paris when they were blasted by a heavy enemy artillery barrage. Captain Hutcheson worked unceasingly under constant hostile fire while attending to the many casualties lying in the open and along rubble strewn streets. Dr. Hutcheson also rendered aid to a hundred or so enemy wounded left behind by the Germans.

A few weeks later Captain Hucheson earned his Victoria Cross. The event occurred on September 2nd when 75th Battalion suffered many wounded while forging through the DQ Support Line. Captain Hutcheson remained in the field until every casualty received care. After dressing the wounds of a seriously injured officer while under intense machinegun and

Contempt for Danger

artillery fire, Hutcheson assisted stretcher bearers transport the officer to the rear. No sooner had he returned to the battlefront when Captain Hutcheson rushed forward in full view of the enemy to reach a wounded sergeant. He relocated the sergeant into the comparative safety of a shell-hole and dressed his injuries. Following the war Bell Hutcheson married a wartime nurse from Nova Scotia. Doctor Hutcheson and his wife raised a son at their home in Cairo, Illinois. The brave doctor died of cancer in 1954 at age seventy-one.

Stretcher-bearer *John Francis Young* was with 87th Battalion, Quebec Grenadier Guards Regiment when he earned his Victoria Cross. On September 2nd when his company suffered heavy casualties Private Young crept about no-man's land dressing the wounds of the injured. For over an hour he labored under heavy machinegun and rifle fire. On several occasions the twenty-five year old wended his way back to the company to retrieve fresh medical supplies. Later in the day he led other stretcher-bearers onto the battlefield to carry out the wounded.

Walter Rayfield was born at Richmond-on-Thames, England. After completing his education Rayfield immigrated to Canada. He was in the real estate business in Vancouver when war broke out. *Walter Leigh Rayfield* served as a private with 7th Infantry Battalion, British Columbia Regiment. In fighting east of Arras on September 2nd thirty-six year old Rayfield realized he had advanced too far ahead of his company. When Rayfield dropped into a trench to await the arrival of the rest of his unit he was confronted by a dozen

108

Hindenburg Line

incredulous Germans. Private Rayfield bayoneted two Germans before the other ten surrendered. He later used his tracking skills to ferret out an enemy sharpshooter who had been sniping at Canadians. Private Rayfield rushed the trench where he last saw the sniper operating. His sudden appearance so startled thirty Germans nestled in the trench they promptly surrendered to him. A couple of days later Rayfield left a safe area to bring in a badly wounded buddy lying on the battlefield. Private Walter Leigh Rayfield was awarded the Victoria Cross for bravery exhibited September 2, 3 and 4, 1918. He spent some time in hospitals after the war recovering from battle wounds. Following an unsuccessful run for Parliament, Rayfield moved to Toronto where he served as Sergeant-at-Arms in the Ontario Legislature. He next pursued a career in reformatory work, latterly rising to the position of governor of Toronto's Don Jail. Walter Rayfield died in 1949 at age 68.

After successfully breaking through the DQ Line, the CEF's next challenge was crossing a one hundred yard wide waterway, the Canal du Nord.

21
Canal du Nord

The concrete sides of Canal du Nord were slathered in slime. A heavily dug-in enemy awaited the Canadians on the far side.

General Arthur Currie sent two assault divisions through a narrow strip of relatively dry ground to broach the network of canals surrounding the city of Cambrai. Canadian shock troops smashed through German defenses then fanned out. The penetration was twenty-five miles deep. A massive flow of tanks, artillery and materiel followed in the wake of the Canadian invaders.

Sam Honey was born in Conn, Ontario. Honey taught school on the Six Nations Indian reserve before enrolling in London Normal School, a teachers training college. Sam Honey was a teacher at Bloomington Elementary School in York County when war broke out. He joined the army as a private in January 1915. Following the battle of Vimy Ridge Sam Honey became a commissioned officer. Second lieutenant Honey was a platoon leader with 78th Battalion, Manitoba Regiment on September 21, 1918 when all the officers of his company except himself were killed or wounded in a firefight near Bourlon Wood, France.

Lieutenant Honey assumed command of the remnants of his company and led it toward its objective. When they bogged

110

Canal du Nord

down under heavy fire Lieutenant Honey personally reconnoitered the situation. After locating the machineguns causing so many casualties he personally rushed the post, captured the guns and returned with ten prisoners in tow. Later, after repelling four enemy counterattacks, Lieutenant Honey captured another machinegun post. He continued to lead his company despite several wounds. Lieutenant Samuel Lewis Honey succumbed to his injuries on the final day of the attack. The twenty-four year old had already earned the Distinguished Conduct Medal and the Military Medal. His Victoria Cross was awarded posthumously. Sam Honey was one of eight hundred and fifty Ontario teachers to serve in the Great War, of whom 101 were slain and another 210 wounded in action.

George Fraser Kerr was born in Deseronto, Ontario in 1894. He joined the army as a private in 1914, went overseas in 1915 and was commissioned a second-lieutenant with 3rd Infantry Battalion, Toronto Regiment. Lieutenant Kerr earned the Military Medal in 1916 for taking command of his platoon while under heavy fire after both the commanding officer and sergeant major were killed. He won the Military Cross in the battle of Amiens in August 1918 after destroying several enemy machinegun positions and capturing two artillery pieces while wounded. A month later, Fraser Kerr was awarded a bar for his Military Cross after knocking out a German machinegun post. Lieutenant Kerr was recuperating from a bullet wound to his arm when his regiment went on the attack. Despite his wound Lieutenant Kerr led his company into battle. When they

Contempt for Danger

encountered a German machinegun blocking their advance at Bourlon Wood near the Canal du Nord Lieutenant Kerr set out on his own and outflanked the German machinegun that had been spraying his platoon. While his company remained pinned down twenty-four year old Fraser Kerr rushed the strong point and single-handedly captured four guns and thirty-one prisoners. Kerr had attained the rank of captain when he was awarded his Victoria Cross by King George V on May 22, 1919. Upon his return to Canada Fraser Kerr went into business for himself. In 1929 George Fraser Kerr was accidentally killed in Toronto.

After receiving a medical discharge from the Royal Navy owing to a recurring ear infection Manchester born *Graham Lyall* immigrated to Canada. He settled near Welland, Ontario. He was working with Niagara Power in St. Catharines when war was declared. Graham enlisted in 1914 and shipped overseas in the spring of 1916. The following year he earned a battlefield commission with the 4th Canadian Mounted Rifles at Vimy Ridge. After completing officer training school in England, Lieutenant Graham returned to the front with 102nd Battalion, 2nd Central Ontario Regiment. On September 27th Lieutenant Graham Lyall led his platoon in the capture of a German artillery piece, four machineguns, and 13 prisoners. Later in the day the twenty-six year old led his weakened platoon against yet another enemy strong point. He rushed forward alone and killed a German officer. Single-handedly he captured 45 prisoners and five machineguns. The completion of his platoon's final objective that day resulted in the capture

112

Canal du Nord

of 41 more prisoners. Four days later, on October 1st, Lieutenant Lyall's under-strength company overran a strongly held position near Blecourt where they captured 60 Germans and 17 machineguns. Graham Thomson Lyall was awarded the Victoria Cross for courageous action in the face of the enemy at the Canal du Nord. Following the Great War Graham Lyall settled in Airdrie, Scotland where he eventually became managing director of a construction company. A major in the British reserve army throughout the 1930s, he was promoted to lieutenant colonel at the outbreak of the Second World War. Graham Lyall was a full colonel when killed in action at Mersa Matruh, Egypt on November 28, 1941.

Milton Gregg was born in Mountain Dale, New Brunswick in 1892. He was a school teacher when war broke out. Milton served with the 13th Infantry Battalion before transferring to the Royal Canadian Regiment. On September 28, 1918 twenty-six year old Lieutenant Gregg led an attack near Cambrai, France which resulted in the surrender of forty-eight Germans including three officers. Shortly after, Gregg was wounded while fighting off a German counterattack. Ignoring his injuries, Lieutenant Gregg led his men into a counterattack of their own. They shot eleven Germans, captured another twenty-five and took possession of twelve enemy machineguns. Gregg was awarded the Victoria Cross for bravery and leadership. A few days later Lieutenant Gregg was severely wounded and had to be evacuated. He remained in the army, subsequently rising in rank to brigadier general. In addition to his VC, Milton Gregg earned a DBE, and Military

Contempt for Danger

Cross with bar. After leaving the service he became a university chancellor, cabinet minister and diplomat before yielding to retirement. Milton Fowler Gregg died in 1978. He was 86.

Canadian troops successfully crossed the Canal du Nord on September 27, 1918.

22
Mons, France

Canada's Expeditionary Force went on to fight at Cambrais, Fort Mount Houey, Valenciennes and Mons before the war ended.

Scottish/Canadian *John MacGregor* was a company commander with 2nd Canadian Mounted Rifles, 1st Central Ontario Regiment. In referring to the five days September 29 through October 3, 1918 his Victoria Cross citation said *Captain MacGregor acted with most conspicuous bravery and leadership* in actions near Cambrai, France. Although wounded, Captain MacGregor led his company through intense enemy fire to put the machineguns out of action that had been peppering his battalion. In taking-out the first gun MacGregor's company killed four Germans and snagged eight prisoners. Captain MacGregor quickly reorganized his command and, in the face of stubborn enemy resistance, resumed his advance. Next morning the twenty-nine year old company commander personally reconnoitered the situation while under constant fire. His forceful advance into Neuville St. Remy was acknowledged to have opened the way for a larger Canadian push all the way to Tilloy. In addition to his Victoria Cross, John MacGregor earned the Military Cross with bar. He later attained the rank of lieutenant colonel. John MacGregor eventually retired to British Columbia and is buried in Powell River.

Contempt for Danger

Twenty-seven-year-old *Sergeant Bill Merrifield* of 4th Battalion, 1st Central Ontario Regiment single-handedly attacked two machinegun emplacements near Abancourt, France. Darting from shell hole to shell hole Merrifield reached the gun pinning down his platoon. He killed the occupants and, although wounded, dashed to a second machinegun post, disabling it with a hand-grenade. Sergeant William Merrifield refused to be evacuated. He continued to lead his platoon until felled by a more severe wound. In addition to his Victoria Cross, Sergeant Merrifield earned the Military Medal.

During the night of October 8th *Captain Coulson Mitchell* commanded a small unit of the 1st Tunneling Company, 4th Canadian Engineer Regiment operating northeast of Cambrai. Their orders were to examine bridges and when possible to prevent their demolition. The twenty-eight year-old captain managed to cut several lead wires on a bridge in total darkness. Then he and a sergeant ran across a second bridge. On the far side Captain Mitchell began cutting wires on the second span leaving his sergeant to stand look out. The enemy attacked and the sergeant fell wounded. Captain Mitchell darted to the sergeant's side, shot three Germans and took another twelve prisoner. Before evacuating the area Captain Mitchell finished cutting the wires and removed the charges. In addition to his Victoria Cross, Coulson Norman Mitchell earned a Military Cross. He later attained the rank of lieutenant colonel.

Canadian troops captured Cambrai on October 9th. The CEF immediately marshaled its resources and advanced on the

Mons, France

fort at Mount Houey. The fort was perched atop a one hundred and fifty foot high hill near Valenciennes.

Wallace Lloyd Algie was born in the Ontario community of Alton in 1891. Wallace was commissioned as an officer in 20th Battalion, 1st Central Ontario Regiment in 1916. Two years later, in October 1918, Lieutenant Algie's unit was held up by machinegun fire emanating from a village on the Canal de l'Escault not far from Cambrais. Supported by nine volunteers Lieutenant Algie raced to the first enemy machinegun, shot the crew, and then turned the gun on the enemy. Meanwhile his unit of volunteers slipped into the village. The lieutenant rushed a second machinegun, killed its crew and captured eleven Germans including an officer. The village was cleared of enemy machineguns. Lieutenant Wallace Lloyd Algie was leading reinforcements up to the village when he was shot and killed by an enemy sniper. This brave Victoria Cross recipient is buried in Niagara Cemetery at Iwuy, France.

Tommie Ricketts grew up in the White Bay fishing community of Middle Arm, Newfoundland. He was only fifteen when he lied about his age and joined the Royal Newfoundland Regiment in 1916. A year later, Tommie was bound for Britain aboard the SS Florizel. By June of 1917 he was at the front. Five months after his arrival, however, he was back in England recovering from gun shot wounds suffered in battle near Cambrai. Private Ricketts did not return to the front until April of the following year. On October 18, 1918 his unit was held up at Ledgehem, Belgium by fierce hostile fire. Ricketts volunteered to advance with his section commander in an

Contempt for Danger

attempt to outflank the enemy pillboxes that had decimated their platoon. Their ammunition ran out 300 yards short of their objective. Ricketts was under constant enemy fire as he scrambled back to the British line to retrieve ammunition for their Lewis gun. Once back in position Ricketts' accurate fire caused the enemy to back-off. This enabled the remnants of Ricketts' platoon to move up without taking further casualties. They captured four field-guns, four machineguns and took eight Germans prisoner. Ricketts' Victoria Cross citation reads in part: *By his presence of mind in anticipating the enemy intention and his utter disregard for personal safety, Private Ricketts secured the further supply of ammunition which directly resulted in these important captures and undoubtedly saved many lives.* Seventeen year old Ricketts was promoted to sergeant and on January 18, 1919 personally received his Victoria Cross from the King at Sandringham Palace. His past bravery had already earned him the right to wear the Croix de Guerre and Distinguished Conduct medals. Upon his return to Newfoundland Thomas Ricketts resumed his schooling. He married and became a pharmacist. Income earned from his drug store in St. John's helped the young couple raise two children. The famous Newfoundlander died in 1967, at age 65.

Twenty-one year old *Hugh Cairns* was the last Canadian recipient of the Victoria Cross during the Great War. Hugh was born in England and raised in Saskatoon, Saskatchewan. He was an apprentice plumber and an active football player when he enlisted in 1915 at the age of nineteen. Hugh Cairns earned the Distinguished Conduct Medal for bravery at Vimy Ridge in

Mons, France

1917. He was a sergeant in the 46th South Saskatchewan Battalion near Valenciennes, France on November 1, 1918 when a German machinegun opened fire on his platoon. Sergeant Cairns grabbed a Lewis gun and rushed the enemy post, killing its crew of five and capturing the gun. Later he captured two more guns, killing a dozen Germans and taking eighteen more prisoner. Although wounded, Sergeant Cairns led a small unit on a flanking movement resulting in the capture of several enemy artillery pieces and machineguns. After consolidating their position, Sergeant Cairns went out on patrol to nearby Marly where he was severely wounded during the capture of sixty Germans. Hugh Cairns died of his wounds the following day, November 2, 1918. His Victoria Cross was awarded posthumously. His brother Albert Cairns, serving with the 65th Saskatchewan Regiment was killed weeks earlier. In 1921 the Saskatoon Football Association erected a statue of Hugh Cairns decked out in football gear. The city park memorial also contains the names of seventy-five other football players who failed to return from the war in Europe. In 1936 the French Government awarded Hugh Cairns the Legion of Honor and the town of Valenciennes named a street after him. Saskatoon did likewise in 1960.

On November 8th the Canadian Expeditionary Force took Valenciennes, a city of 30,000 people. Later that day the CEF liberated Mons. At the nearby village of Ville-sur-Haine three days later George Price was felled by a German sniper's bullet. Price was the 60,661st and last Canadian to be killed in action during the Great War. He was shot at 10:58 am. Two minutes

Contempt for Danger

later the war officially ended; at the eleventh hour of the eleventh day of the eleventh month - November 11, 1918.

Of the more than six hundred thousand who donned a Canadian military uniform during the Great War, 60,661 were killed, and another 172,000 wounded. At war's end 418,000 Canadian soldiers were still stationed in Europe. Of the 23,000 Canadians to serve with the British air services (the Royal Flying Corps and Royal Navy Air Service), 1,563 lost their lives.

Seventy-one courageous Canadian servicemen and Canadians serving in other Commonwealth units earned the Victoria Cross, the British Empire's highest award for valor.

Mons, France

Great War
Victoria Cross Honor Roll

Lieutenant Wallace L. Algie	Army	Cambrai, France 1918
Major William G. Barker	Air Force	Foret de Mormal, France 1918
Corporal Colin F. Barron	Army	Passchendaele, Belgium 1917
Lieutenant Edward D. Bellew	Army	Kerselaere, Belgium 1915
Lieutenant-Colonel Philip E. Bent	Army	Polygon Wood, Belgium 1917
Captain William A. Bishop	Air Force	Cambrai, France 1917
Lieutenant Roland R. Bourke	Navy	Ostend, Belgium 1918
Corporal Alexander P. Brereton	Army	Amiens, France 1918
Lieutenant Jean Brillant	Army	Meharicourt, France 1918
Private Harry Brown	Army	Loos, France 1917
Sergeant Hugh Cairns	Army	Valenciennes, France 1918
Lieutenant Frederick W. Campbell	Army	Givenchy, France 1915
Corporal Leo Clarke	Army	Pozieres, France 1916
Lieut-Colonel William Clark-Kennedy	Army	Fresnes, France 1918
Lieutenant Robert G. Combe	Army	Acheville, France 1917
Corporal Frederick G. Coppins	Army	Hackett Woods, France 1918
Private John B. Croak	Army	Amiens, France 1918
Private Robert E. Cruickshank	Army	Jordan, Palestine 1918
Second Lieutenant Edmund De Wind	Army	Groagie, France 1918
Private Thomas Dinesen	Army	Parvillers, France 1918
Lance Corporal Frederick Fisher	Army	St. Julien, Belgium 1915
Lieutenant Gordon M. Flowerdew	Army	Bois de Moreuil, France 1918
Corporal Herman J. Good	Army	Hangard Wood, France 1918
Lieutenant Milton F. Gregg	Army	Cambrai, France 1918
Sergeant Major Frederick W. Hall	Army	Ypres, Belgium 1915

Contempt for Danger

Sergeant Major Robert H. Hanna	Army	Lens, France 1917
Lieutenant Frederick M. Harvey	Army	Guyencourt, France 1917
Sergeant Frederick Hobson	Army	Lens, France 1917
Private Thomas W. Holmes	Army	Passchendaele, Belgium 1917
Lieutenant Samuel L. Honey	Army	Bourlon Wood, France 1918
Captain Bellenden S. Hutcheson	Army	Queant Drocourt, France 1918
Corporal Joseph Kaeble	Army	Neuville-Vitasse, France 1918
Lieutenant George F. Kerr	Army	Bourlon Wood, France 1918
Private John C. Kerr	Army	Courcelette, France 1916
Private Cecil J. Kinross	Army	Passchendaele, Belgium 1917
Sergeant Arthur G. Knight	Army	Villers les Cagnicourt, France 1918
Corporal Filip Konowal	Army	Lens, France 1917
Major Okill M. Learmonth	Army	Loos, France 1917
Lieutenant Graham T. Lyall	Army	Cambrai, France 1918
Captain Thain W. MacDowell	Army	Vimy Ridge, France 1917
Captain John MacGregor	Army	Cambrai, France 1918
Lieutenant George B. McKean	Army	Gavrelle Sector, France 1918
Lieutenant Hugh McKenzie	Army	Meetscheele Spur, Belgium 1917
Second Lieutenant Alan A. McLeod	Air Force	Albert, France 1918
Sergeant William Merrifield	Army	Abancourt, France 1918
Corporal William H. Metcalf	Army	Arras, France 1918
Private William J. Milne	Army	Thelus, France 1917
Corporal Harry G. Miner	Army	Demuin, France 1918
Captain Coulson N. Mitchell	Army	Canal de L'Escaut, France 1918
Sergeant George H. Mullin	Army	Passchendaele, Belgium 1917
Private Claude J. Nunney	Army	Drocourt-Queant Line, France 1918
Captain Christopher P. O'Kelly	Army	Passchendaele, Belgium 1917
Lance Corporal Michael O'Leary	Army	Cuinchy, France 1915

Mons, France

Private Michael J. O'Rourke	Army	Hill 60, France 1917
Private John G. Pattison	Army	Vimy Ridge, France 1917
Major George R. Pearkes	Army	Passchendaele, Belgium 1917
Lieutenant-Colonel Cyrus W. Peck	Army	Cagnicourt, France 1918
Private Walter L. Rayfield	Army	Arras, France 1918
Piper James C. Richardson	Army	Somme, France 1916
Private James P. Robertson	Army	Passchendaele, Belgium 1917
Lieutenant Charles S. Rutherford	Army	Monchy, France 1918
Captain Francis A. Scrimger	Army	St. Julien, Belgium 1915
Lieutenant Robert Shankland	Army	Passchendaele, Belgium 1917
Sergeant Ellis W. Sifton	Army	Neuville-St. Vaast, France 1917
Captain John A. Sinton	Army	Orah Ruins, Mesopotamia 1916
Sergeant Robert Spall	Army	Parvillers, France 1918
Lieutenant Harcus Strachan	Army	Masnieres, France 1917
Lieutenant James E. Tait	Army	Amiens, France 1918
Lieutenant Thomas O. Wilkinson	Army	La Boiselle, France 1916
Private John F. Young	Army	Dury-Arras Sector, France 1918
Sergeant Raphael L. Zengel	Army	Warvillers, France 1918

23
Peace

Before the Great War ended, both Russia and Ireland were embroiled in the throes of violent internal strife. The War Office in Ottawa did nothing concerning Ireland but in October 1918 ordered 4,000 Canadian troops to Vladivostok to assist Allied efforts in protecting the Russian seaport. Seven Canadians died in action before the Canadian Siberian Brigade was withdrawn and returned home in 1919.

The Russian revolution ended in 1920. The following year the Irish Free State was born, uniting all of Ireland except sixteen counties in the north.

With the formation of its own air force in 1924, Canada's armed forces had evolved into three distinctive military arms - the Royal Canadian Army, Royal Canadian Navy and the Royal Canadian Air Force. The navy may well have thought the new air force had been created at their expense when, in the following year, Canada's fifteen year old military sea arm reeled from the impact of severe budgetary cuts. In a wink Canada's peace time navy was reduced to a single cruiser, two destroyers and two submarines. Further, the new Naval College in Halifax was permanently shut down.

Plummeting prices on the New York Stock Exchange in October of 1929 was the harbinger of a worldwide financial market meltdown. Prices on the Toronto and Montreal

Peace

exchanges fell in the worst free fall in Canadian financial history. The *Great Depression* had begun. At its height, one and a half million Canadians were without work. Eight years would elapse before any significant amelioration in unemployment levels could be observed. And it would take ten years for the crippling depression to end.

In January 1933 two leaders of dramatically different persuasions ascended to power - Franklin Roosevelt as president of the United States, and Adolf Hitler as chancellor of Germany. Both would die twelve years later, in April 1945, each having left an indelible imprint on their respective nations and the world.

In July 1936 King Edward VIII unveiled the *Vimy Ridge Memorial* in France commemorating the more than sixty-thousand Canadians killed during the Great War. The monument, designed by Toronto sculptor Walter Allward, had taken eleven years to construct.

The number of Canadians unemployed and on relief in 1937 shrank to 1.3 million; 200,000 fewer than the previous year.

Addressing a crowd at Kingston, Ontario on August 18, 1938 President Franklin D. Roosevelt assured Canadians the United States would not stand idly by in the event Canada was invaded by a foreign power.

In the following year the Spanish Civil War ended with the capture of Madrid by troops of Generalissimo Franco. German and Italian armed forces had used Spain as a virtual military training experiment in their support of Franco's bid to install a

125

Contempt for Danger

fascist government. Inside of three years 300,000 Spaniards had perished. Most of the 1,300 Canadian volunteers who fought in the Spanish Civil War marched with the Mackenzie-Papineau Battalion, International Brigade. Almost half were slain. The Canadian battalion was named in honor of the country's two most famous patriots of the 1837 rebellions – William Lyon Mackenzie and Louis Papineau.

By 1939 Canada had become home to eleven million people. The young nation consisted of nine provinces and three territories. Newfoundland did not join Canadian Confederation until 1949 and Nunavuk Territory had yet to be conceived.

The Dominion of Canada, as the nation was officially known from 1867 through 1982, had neither a flag of its own nor a national anthem. Until the introduction of the maple leaf flag in 1965, Canadian Forces marched under the *Red Ensign* - a red banner featuring a union jack in the upper left corner opposite Canada's coat-of-arms. And until *O Canada* was designated the nation's official anthem in 1980, Canadian events were usually heralded with a stirring rendition of one of two patriotic songs - *the Maple Leaf Forever* or *O Canada*.

In June of 1939 King George VI, accompanied by his wife Queen Elizabeth, became the first reigning monarch to visit Canada. Everywhere the king and queen traveled across the nation they were warmly greeted by vast crowds of cheering Canadians. Prior to departing Canada for their planned visit to Washington and New York City, the royal couple took time to open Canada's first four-lane highway - Ontario's *Queen Elizabeth Way*.

126

Peace

Apart from Remembrance Day Services on November 11th, most citizens had been content to simply forget about war. The media, intellectuals and academia popularly referred to the Great War as *the war to end all wars*. Obviously the federal government believed this to be the case because when war came in 1939 Canada was ill prepared.

And with the advent of the latest war, the expression *War to End All Wars* faded into disuse, soon to be superceded by a more apt designation, *World War I*.

25
Signs of the Times

Despite widespread financial hardship inflicted by the Depression, life in Canada during the 1930's was in many respects easier than in the years immediately preceding World War I. Horse drawn trolleys had given way to electric powered streetcars. Buses competed with steam powered locomotives for passengers in the expanding inter city transportation market. Network radio was emerging as a primary form of family entertainment. Silent films had been relegated to history, replaced by full length audio enhanced movies; some filmed in color.

Almost forty percent of Canadian households now had a telephone. Multi-party telephone service was popular in rural exchanges particularly those linked to ten or more customers sharing the same phone line. Incoming calls rang simultaneously in the homes of all ten party-line customers, leaving it up to the designated party to recognize their own distinctive ring code – such as *two long, one short*. Residential phone lines in urban communities were usually a *two-party* service line with incoming calls ringing only in the home of the designated recipient.

Cities were dependent on buses and electric-powered streetcars as prime movers of people as there were no rapid-transit systems in Canada in the 1930s. For twenty-five

Signs of the Times

cents public transit riders in Toronto could purchase four adult or ten child fares. Newspapers were available six days a week, usually at 3 cents per copy; same price for home delivery.

Home delivery service was popular for more than newspapers. Horse and wagons of competing bread companies plied urban streets daily. Horse drawn wagons also delivered milk and ice. It took a pair of draft horses to haul a load of weighty bags of coal. Drivers of privately-owned horse drawn carts retrieved junk discarded at curbside. Householders put-out *ash cans and trashcans* as most urban dwellings were heated by coal-fired furnaces.

Many legendary emporium icons of 1939 have since faded from existence – Creeds, Dupuis Freres, Eaton's, A.J. Frieman, Kresges, Morgan's, Simpsons, Woolworths, Woodwards. Fleets of department store trucks delivered customer purchases to city residences Monday through Saturday; with some locales receiving twice daily deliveries. Brewery company trucks delivered beer to private homes. Letter postage was 3 cents for in-town delivery, 4 cents for out-of-town service. Letter carriers plied their routes twice daily Monday through Friday, plus once on Saturdays.

Adult moviegoers could view two feature films, world-news, a cartoon, and oftentimes *a movie short* for twenty-five cents at a neighborhood theater. On Saturday matinees children paid twelve cents to watch two movies, world-news, three cartoons, plus the latest episode of a weekly serial.

Municipal governments tended to restrict gasoline purchases to twelve hours a day, typically 7am to 7pm. On a

Contempt for Danger

rotation basis designated service stations opened for business Sunday afternoons.

City dwellers financially able to escape summer's heat and humidity might rent a waterfront cottage. Interiors of their rustic abodes were generally unfinished; resulting in exposed wall studs, few interior doors, and no ceiling between floor and roof. Pails of drinking water had to be fetched from a neighborhood well or spring. Water for washing-purposes was hauled from a nearby lake or river. A one or two-hole wooden outhouse served as the cottage privy. Indoor nighttime lighting was often by kerosene lamp or candle. And a wood stove was typically the primary source of warmth on chilly evenings.

Quebec was known for its liberal laws regarding the consumption of alcoholic spirits; similar in many respects to New York State regulations. By contrast, Ontario obliged prospective purchasers of bottled liquor to be 21 years of age, possess a valid Ontario Liquor Permit, and complete a written purchase order at a government operated retail liquor outlet. Inside the government emporium customers dutifully identified brand names and inventory numbers from listings posted on a wall and transcribed this vital data along with his/her permit number, name and signature onto a government order-form. Permit, order-form and money were presented to a cashier. After paying for their purchase the buyer then presented their *cashier-endorsed order-form* to a filling-clerk. The clerk disappeared into a mysterious back room, returning moments later with the specified item(s),

130

Signs of the Times

which was shown to the customer for approval before being quickly tucked into a brown paper bag.

Outside of Quebec which allowed taverns, the most popular locale to publicly consume a cold glass of beer was at a beverage room, commonly called a *beer parlor*. Many beer parlors featured two entrances, one designated *men only*, the other labeled *ladies and escorts*. Only males over 21 years of age were legally permitted to enter the *men only* door. Only women or a man in the company of a woman were allowed to enter a *ladies and escorts* entrance. Licensed establishments opened six days a week from noon to two pm, 4pm to 6:30, and from 8 o'clock to last call at 11:30pm.

Quebec was also the most tolerant of Sunday activities. By way of contrast, Ontario patrons of beer parlors, bowling alleys, bingo halls, and movie theaters were expected to exit the premises by midnight on Saturdays. As Sunday was considered a day of rest, theaters remained closed and no commercial sporting activity was countenanced.

24
Call to Arms

Germany's sudden occupation of the Saar and Alsace-Lorraine demilitarized zones bordering France clearly contravened the Treaty of Versailles yet went uncontested. Two years later, in March of 1938, 'The Third Reich', as the National Socialist Party or *Nazis* preferred to identify their nation, annexed Austria. Seven months later German troops marched into the Sudetenland sector of Czechoslovakia.

The night of November 9, 1938 became known throughout the world as *'Kristalnacht'* owing to tons of shattered glass smashed from Jewish storefronts in race riots across Germany. Ninety people died during the systematic destruction of Jewish homes, businesses and synagogues. The wide scale assault, looting, and arson on Kristalnacht was manipulated by the Nazis following a public broadcast that a Polish Jew had murdered a German diplomat in Paris.

German troops marching into Prague on March 15, 1939 caught British and French leaders unprepared. A Peace Pact endorsed by the leaders of Britain, France, and Germany plus Benito Mussolini of Italy in Munich scarcely a year earlier was intended to contain German encroachment of Czechoslovakian territory to the Sudetenland. Apparently it had not.

Call to Arms

While the American film classic *'Gone With the Wind'* was reaping world acclaim, the USSR and Germany announced the signing of a non-aggression pact on August 23rd 1939. Poland lay between the two former archenemies, the Soviet Union and the Third Reich. As an expression of concern over Poland's future, Britain and France publicly reaffirmed their commitment to come to Poland's aid in the event of foreign attack. Such an attack came within days. On Friday September 1st German troops smashed across Polish borders. Anglo/French ultimatums issued to the Chancellor of the Third Reich demanding immediate withdrawal of German troops or expect total war went unanswered.

Sunday September 3, 1939 British Prime Minister Neville Chamberlain announced a state of war existed between Great Britain and Germany. Within hours a U-boat – German submarine - torpedoed the British liner *SS Athenia* off the coast of Scotland.

A week later on September 10, *Canada declared war on the German Reich*. Opposition Parties lent their support to the Bill after the Government agreed that Canadian conscripts would not be sent overseas unless they specifically volunteered for *General Service*.

Poland succumbed within thirty days, but not before Soviet troops marched across its virtually undefended eastern frontier. The world now realized the extent of Germany's incentive to the USSR in exchange for signing a non-aggression pact the previous month.

Contempt for Danger

A daring U-boat raid on the huge British naval base at Scapa Flow resulted in the sinking of the battleship HMS Royal Oak. In November Soviet planes bombed Viipuri and Helsinki, Finland in a prelude to Soviet ground *invasion*.

Canada was unprepared for war. Most equipment available to Canada's small standing army of about 4,500 and partially trained militia was outdated. The navy had 1,700 men and only thirteen ships - six destroyers, four minesweepers, two training schooners and a trawler. The nation's tiny air force flew aging aircraft. Because no one really expected the war to last long - perhaps several months, a year at most - the government believed Canada's contribution to the war effort would be largely military materiel, augmented by small numbers of personnel. Nevertheless, men were obliged to register with the newly formed *National Selective Service* agency.

Thousands rushed to enlist in the armed forces where recruits were paid $1.30 a day. Volunteers thronged from every province and territory. Most were exceptionally fit, eager young men. There were lawyers, doctors, businessmen, farmers, educators, teamsters and the temporarily unemployed. Some had a university degree, many were high school graduates, others had not graduated from elementary school. Many volunteers had never seen an airplane; most had not seen an ocean-going ship. Indeed, the majority of young volunteers had never ventured more than twenty miles beyond their home.

Canada was scarcely seventy-two years old when the Second World War broke out. Her army had seen service in

Call to Arms

Canada's Northwest Rebellion, the British Boer War, and in the Great War. Canada's navy had been created in 1910 just in time to play a minor role in the Great War. Only Canada's air force, which wasn't formed until 1924, was yet to be bloodied.

Canadian *Major General Andrew McNaughton*, a national hero in the Great War, was appointed commander of Canada's expeditionary force. In November advance elements of *1st Canadian Division* began to arrive in England.

Under the newly formed *British Commonwealth Air Training Program* aircrew throughout the British Commonwealth were to be trained in Canada.

At the outset of the war Canadian firms owned no engineering designs for heavy weapons. As a result the Canadian Navy sent unarmed warships to Britain with gray painted telegraph poles fitted into wooden deck mounts to simulate armament. The utility pole shams were replaced with real deck guns when the Canadian-built ships reached British ports.

On November 1, *Trans Canada Airlines* initiated coast-to-coast air service. Also that month the Supreme Court of Canada upheld the right of Quebec tavern owners to decline service to black persons. At the time Canada's armed forces were still refusing to enlist people of color even though the army had done so in the midst of the Great War.

By February 1940, 23,000 Canadian troops had been safely convoyed to Britain for training by the Royal Army at Aldershot in the south of England. #110 Fighter Squadron was the first of many Canadian squadrons to reach the British Isles.

Contempt for Danger

In March of 1940 Finland and the USSR signed a peace accord. Weeks later German forces suddenly and without warning smashed into Denmark and Norway. Belgium and Holland had declared their neutrality yet in May the German war machine attacked Holland, Belgium and Luxembourg. British Prime Minister Neville Chamberlain resigned in disgrace when it became obvious his policy of appeasement had utterly failed. Chamberlain was succeeded by a coalition government led by Winston Churchill.

When the German army overran Denmark and most of Norway, two Canadian infantry brigades were designated to assist the British Army in Norway. However, before most could ship-out from Scotland fresh orders directed them to return to Aldershot. Scandinavia had been lost! Six hundred and fifty Canadian troops did land at Spitzbergen where, to deny fuel to German industry, they set fire to 500,000 tons of Norwegian coal before withdrawing.

Already reeling from the ferocity of the German onslaught the Allies were further knocked off-stride by the sudden collapse of Belgium. The British Expeditionary Force and several French divisions were cut-off from the core of the French Army by an unexpectedly powerful thrust of panzers - German tank armies. In early June, 338,000 British and French troops were safely evacuated to England through the French seaport of Dunkirk.

Yet a few days later, on June 4, the Royal Air Force ordered *#242 Canadian Fighter Squadron* to France only to hurriedly withdraw it two weeks later. On June 13th a Canadian infantry

Call to Arms

brigade landed in France with orders to form a defensive line across the Brittany Peninsula. Three days later they too retreated to Britain, bringing back most all of their equipment. Later that month Canadian Navy destroyer *Fraser* was sunk

Italy suddenly attacked southern France and declared war on Great Britain. Paris fell on June 14. Already on the verge of capitulation, France was now obliged to seek peace with two belligerents, Germany and Italy.

An Axis/French peace protocol was endorsed by high ranking German and French officials in a railroad coach at Compeigne, France; the scene of the signing of the armistice ending the Great War twenty-two years earlier. Northern France, to be known as Frankreich, would remain under German occupation. Vichy, comprising southern France and Algeria, was to become a German protectorate. Germany allowed Italy to retain the Riviera, the small portion of south France its troops had captured.

The *Axis* was a mutual assistance pact formed by the Third Reich and Italy in 1936. Originally known as the *Rome-Berlin Axis* the cabal was expanded four years later with the admittance of the Empire of Japan. Japan had annexed Korea early in the century, marched into Manchuria in 1933 and, since 1937 had been striving to conquer China.

The British Channel Islands fell to the Germans in July, the same month the USSR completed its occupation of the Baltic States – Estonia, Latvia and Lithuania. To avoid its falling into German hands the Royal Navy destroyed a portion of the French naval fleet anchored in Algerian ports.

26
Opening Salvos

In July 1940 Andy McNaughton was promoted to lieutenant general and given command of Anglo/Canadian 7th Corps. By month's end advance elements of *2nd Canadian Division* began to arrive in England; the remainder were not scheduled to follow until December.

With the cessation of fighting on the Continent, the German victors directed their attention toward Great Britain. The *Luftwaffe* - Germany's air force - launched the *Battle of Britain* with the bombing of Royal Air Force (RAF) airfields and radar installations. The first battle engagement ever fought by Canada's new air force occurred when Hawker Hurricanes of *#1 Canadian Fighter Squadron* joined the Battle of Britain in early August. Within weeks the #242 Canadian Fighter Squadron also joined the battle. *Pilot Officer D.A. Hewitt* was the first Canadian flyer to be killed. Of 110 Canadian pilots who fought in the historic battle three were awarded the Distinguished Flying Cross.

Prior to graduating to mainline battle aircraft, such as Hurricanes or Spitfires, aspiring Canadian fighter pilots earned their wings by completing twenty-two weeks of training at one of Canada's ninety-seven flight training centers. Invariably the first plane they flew was a 145 horsepower *Tiger Moth* bi-plane. Most cadets progressed to the *North American Harvard*, an all

Opening Salvos

metal 600 horsepower trainer capable of 200 miles per hour and soaring to altitudes of 25,000 feet.

Hawker Hurricanes had a metal airframe, metal covered wings, and a fabric–covered fuselage. Armed with eight .30 caliber machineguns, the single-seat fighter could attain altitudes of 34,000 feet and fly at 325 miles per hour. During the war four hundred Hurricanes were built in Canada.

Canadian fighter pilots also flew the Vickers *Supermarine Spitfire*. The highly maneuverable Spitfire was a single seat all-metal fighter capable of attaining speeds exceeding 400 miles per hour. Canadian Spitfires were usually armed with two machine guns and two cannons.

The Luftwaffe switched from military to civilian bombing targets in mid September. From then through year-end British cities and seaports were blitzed by thousands of tons of bombs. On December 29 a third of London was set ablaze in one of the largest raids the historic capital had yet endured. All that autumn a land invasion by German troops seemed imminent. However, before year-end RAF aerial photographs revealed the German armada of landing craft amassed along the French coast had dispersed. The planned invasion of England was apparently cancelled or at least postponed.

In 1938 President Roosevelt had promised Prime Minister King that the United States would not stand idly by in the event Canada's freedom was threatened. Now, two years later Prime Minister Mackenzie King conferred with U.S. President Franklin Roosevelt at Ogdensburg, New York to discuss areas of mutual defense. The national leaders agreed to the formation

Contempt for Danger

of a *Permanent Joint Board on Defense* to oversee the air, sea and land defense of the northern half of the Western Hemisphere. In September Canada took possession of seven old U.S. Navy destroyers under an innovative Anglo/American lend/lease agreement.

In the Pacific the Canadian Navy's armed merchantman *Prince Robert* captured a German ship off the coast of Mexico. In the Atlantic Canadian destroyer *Margaree* was sunk. On October 26th Canadian Pacific liner *Empress of Britain* was torpedoed and sunk. Canadian destroyer *Saguenay*, by contrast, was luckier than both the Margaree and Empress of Britain.

On December 1st, 1940 destroyer Saguenay was on convoy duty west of Ireland when she was torpedoed by the Italian submarine Argo. Twenty-one Canadian sailors died when Saguenay's bow was shorn off. The crippled ship settled low in the water yet did not sink. Fresh out of torpedoes, the Argo surfaced and began shelling the Saguenay. Canadian sailors remained at their battle-stations and returned fire. The Argo quickly submerged. Royal Navy destroyer HMS Highlander took aboard all but a skeleton crew from the faltering Canadian warship. Cruising in reverse, the Saguenay limped slowly to the safety of a British port more than 300 miles distant. **Commander G.R. Miles**, the Saguenay's captain, was decorated for his leadership under fire. Five months later restoration of the Saguenay was completed and she returned to North Atlantic convoy duty.

Under Canada's new *National Resources Mobilization Act* draftees were called-up for homeland defense. Initial

Opening Salvos

home-defense regulations obliged draft-age men to undergo only one month of military training – essentially small arms familiarization and close order drill yet the call-up of Quebecois so incensed *Camillien Houde,* the Mayor of Montreal, he openly encouraged Quebecers to defy the law. When the immensely popular five-foot seven, 250 pound mayor refused to retract his comments he was arrested by the RCMP. For the next four years Camillien Houde was confined to a federal government internment camp. Upon his release in the summer of 1944 Houde, now one hundred pounds lighter, was greeted by thousands of cheering Montrealers. At the next municipal election Houde handily won his fifth term as Mayor of Montreal.

Princess Juliana of the Netherlands, her husband Prince Bernhard and their two young daughters having fled their homeland established residency in Ottawa for the duration of the war. Juliana became Queen of the Netherlands in 1948. She died in 2004 at age 94.

On the legislative scene Quebec extended the voting franchise to women, the last province to do so. At the federal level a new edict obliged immigrants of German and Italian descent, including those naturalized after 1922, to be stripped of Canadian citizenship and register with local authorities as enemy aliens.

By 1940 year's end, the first flotilla of Canadian built *corvettes* sailed for Britain. *Corvettes* became the mainstay of Canada's trans Atlantic convoy escort service. The one thousand ton warship was originally designed for British

Contempt for Danger

coastal defense. Many corvettes were built in shipyards on the Great Lakes. The 210-foot little ships were small enough to use the canal system to bypass the Lachine Rapids on the St. Lawrence River while en route from the Great Lakes to the Atlantic. Corvettes had a top speed of sixteen knots. By maintaining a cruising speed of ten knots they could travel up to 7,400 miles – sufficient to cross the Atlantic and back. Corvettes rolled heavily even in the modest of seas. Their open-bridge was brutal duty for watch-keepers especially in heavy weather. While corvettes were not expected to win battles against larger more conventional classes of warship they proved to be capable submarine chasers. Typically a corvette had a crew of 85 and was armed with a 4-inch gun, an anti-aircraft gun, two 20 mm machineguns, plus seventy or more depth charges.

27
World Conflagration

British forces fared well fighting the Italian army in North Africa until Adolf Hitler ordered Field Marshal Irwin Rommel to reinvigorate the Axis desert campaign. Rommel's innovative and wily tactics earned him the sobriquet *The Desert Fox*. Meanwhile on the north side of the Mediterranean, the *Wehrmacht* - German army - marched into Yugoslavia and Greece to motivate a flagging Italian campaign there.

At a meeting in Hyde Park, New York, Prime Minister Mackenzie King and President Franklin Roosevelt agreed the two nations would closely collaborate in the production of war materiel. The Hyde Park meeting was a follow-through to the *Ogdensburg Agreement* announced the previous year. By May of 1941 tanks and artillery were rolling from Canadian assembly lines. By summer, women were being admitted into the armed forces. Earlier in the year Ottawa extended compulsory military training under the home-defense Mobilization Act from one month to four. Subsequently the term was extended to six months, then one year, eventually *for the duration*.

Seventy-three army personnel were lost in the torpedoing of the Canadian passenger ship Nerissa off the coast of Ireland. On May 27, 1941 the Royal Navy sank Germany's most powerful battleship, the *Bismarck*, off the coast of France.

143

Contempt for Danger

Bismarck had been the target of an intensive North Atlantic hunt following its sinking of the pride of the British navy - battlecruiser HMS Hood with severe loss of life.

Leonard Warren Murray was born in Granton, Nova Scotia in 1896. Len was a member of the first graduating class of the Canadian Naval College in Halifax. He served as a midshipman on Royal Navy ships during World War I. In 1939 Captain Murray was appointed Deputy Chief of Naval Staff in Ottawa. Two years later Murray was promoted to Commodore and given command of the newly created *Northwest Atlantic Escort Force* headquartered at St. John's, Newfoundland. In 1943 Murray was promoted to Rear Admiral and made Commander-in-Chief Northwest Atlantic based in Halifax in charge of all Allied air and naval forces involved in convoy protection. Rear Admiral Murray was the only Canadian appointed to head an Allied theater of operations. After the war Murray retired to England. He was called to the bar in 1949 and practiced law until his retirement. Leonard Murray died in 1971 at age 75.

In mid April 1941 # 402 *Canadian Fighter Squadron* flew its first attack over enemy territory. Within weeks Canadian bombers completed their first raid over Germany. Canadian corvettes sank their first U-boat in September 1941. And in the fall of that year Air Force Eastern Command began attacking U-Boats off the coast of Newfoundland. In other action Canadian corvettes *Levis* and *Windflower* were lost as was the armed-yacht *Otter*.

144

World Conflagration

Although many Canadian bomber aviators earned their wings flying a Harvard trainer, Cadets pre-selected for bomber pilot training often went direct from the Tiger-Moth to a twin-engine Cessna Crane to earn their wings. Initially the main Canadian bomber was the *Vickers Wellington*, nicknamed *the Wimpy*. Wimpys were constructed by stretching a cloth fabric membrane over a metal lattice framework. The twin-engine aircraft had a crew of five. Armed with .30 caliber machineguns front and rear, Wellingtons carried a 2 -1/2 ton bomb load and could fly at 235 miles per hour.

On June 22nd 1941 one hundred German divisions - augmented by troops from Romania and Finland - invaded the Soviet Union along a one thousand mile front. Momentum of the Axis advance continued virtually unabated until the onset of winter ground it to a halt at the outskirts of Leningrad and suburbs of Moscow.

At Britain's urgent request Canada sent two regiments, totaling 1,975 men, to reinforce the British garrison at Hong Kong. Canadian **Colonel J.K. Lawson** was promoted to brigadier general and given command of the brigade comprising two regiments; the Winnipeg Grenadiers and Quebec City Rifles. The Canadian Expeditionary Force disembarked from SS Awaten at the port of Hong Kong November 16th 1941.

In making their request for Canadian assistance the British high command informed Ottawa that, in the event of war with Japan, Japanese military capabilities were considered weak and inefficient. Yet the British never revealed their concern that

145

Contempt for Danger

Hong Kong could not withstand a major assault. The British garrison had no air cover, few mobile artillery pieces and little motor transport. Worse, all their big guns were trained seaward. On Sunday morning December 7th, bomber fleets and fighter squadrons from six Japanese aircraft-carriers bombed and strafed Pearl Harbor, Hawaii.

On December 8th, only three weeks after the Canadian contingent arrived, the Japanese 38th Division invaded Hong Kong from the Chinese mainland. Within ten days the British garrison was suffering from extreme shortages of water, food and medicines, with no prospect of replenishment and no chance of evacuation.

On the outskirts of the city on the morning of December 19th a company of Winnipeg Grenadiers attacked *Mount Butler*, actually a steep hill rising from the sea. Company Sergeant Major John Osborn gave the order to *fix bayonets*. Although only a portion of Osborn's men reached the peak, they successfully captured the hilltop at bayonet point.

Japanese infantry began amassing at the base of Mount Butler. Soon the enemy launched a counterattack in a confident attempt to win back the mountain.

Completely cut off, the Canadians at the peak of Mount Butler held out for three hours before Osborn considered their position untenable. Keeping a small group with him to provide covering fire, Sergeant Major Osborne ordered the rest of his men to withdraw from the hill.

Johnnie Osborn was born in Norfolk England January 2, 1899. As a Royal Navy seaman in World War I Osborn saw

146

World Conflagration

action in May 1916 at the Battle of Jutland. After the war Osborn immigrated to Wapell, Saskatchewan to try his hand at farming. Two years later Osborn moved to Manitoba where he hired on as a maintenance worker with Canadian Pacific Railway. His steady income enabled John Osborn to marry and raise five children. In 1933, at the height of the *Great Depression*, John Osborn enlisted in the Winnipeg Grenadiers reserve. He rose rapidly in rank. Six years later, on September 3, 1939 the Grenadiers were placed on active-duty status. Now Sergeant Major Osborn was fighting for his life atop Mount Butler.

It was time to concede the hill. As the last of his men slid down the incline to relative safety, Osborn single-handedly held off the enemy. The London Gazette explained what followed. *Company Sergeant Major Osborn had to run the gauntlet of heavy rifle and machinegun fire. With no consideration for his own safety he assisted and directed stragglers to the new company position, exposing himself to heavy enemy fire to cover their retirement. Wherever danger threatened he was there to encourage his men.*

By the afternoon of December 19th the situation was dire. The Gazette's report continued: *During the afternoon the company was cut off from the battalion and completely surrounded by the enemy, who were able to approach to within grenade throwing distance of the slight depression which the company was holding. Several enemy grenades were thrown which Company Sergeant Major Osborn picked up and threw back. The enemy threw a grenade, which landed in a position where it was impossible to pick up and return it in time. Shouting a warning to his comrades this gallant*

147

Contempt for Danger

Non-Commissioned Officer threw himself on the grenade, which exploded, killing him instantly. His self-sacrifice undoubtedly saved the lives of many others.

His Victoria Cross citation reads: *Company Sergeant Major Osborn was an inspiring example to all throughout the defense which he assisted so magnificently in maintaining against an overwhelming enemy force for over eight and a half hours, and in his death he displayed the highest quality of heroism and self-sacrifice.* Sergeant Major John Robert Osborn was 42 when he gave his life for his adopted country.

Sergeant Major John Osborne was the first of sixteen Canadians to be awarded the Victoria Cross for heroic action in World War II; nine posthumously. All were born within a span of thirty-two years – 1889 through 1921. The youngest recipient was only twenty-four years of age, the eldest fifty-four. Most were in their twenties or thirties.

At nearby Canadian command headquarters, the situation had become desperate. With a blazing pistol in each hand Brigadier General Lawson charged the Japanese line. The two-gun general was cut down by enemy fire in front of his men. The general's dramatic charge so impressed a Japanese colonel, the colonel ordered the Canadian's body to be wrapped in a Japanese officer's blanket and buried.

Three hundred Canadians were killed in the Japanese assault of Hong Kong, which fell on Christmas Day. Japanese troops murdered hospitalized wounded soldiers, raped the nurses and beat those offering to surrender. Many prisoners witnessed the agonizing deaths of several comrades that

World Conflagration

Japanese soldiers had tied to posts and were using for bayonet practice. The victors marched-off 10,000 Commonwealth troops, including nearly 1,700 Canadians. During 3-1/2 years of Japanese captivity a further 195 Canadians died from malnutrition and lack of basic necessities.

Overnight the United States and the British Commonwealth had been thrust into war with the Empire of Japan. In addition to Hawaii and Hong Kong, Japanese forces attacked Guam, Malaya, the Philippines, Singapore, Thailand and Wake Island. To publicly demonstrate the Third Reich's support for its Axis partner in the Far East, Adolf Hitler declared war on the United States of America.

Within days of the Axis' proclamations, Prime Minister Winston Churchill sailed for North America. The British leader met first with President Roosevelt in Washington where he addressed a joint session of the U.S. Congress. The President's private railroad coaches conveyed Churchill to his next stopover – Ottawa. At the Canadian capital Winston Churchill delivered a rousing speech to a special joint session of Parliament on December 30th.

By year end 1941 the Canadian Navy had 64 corvettes at sea. The Air Force had grown to thirty squadrons; 14 overseas, another 16 based in Canada.

The new year began with Ottawa's announcement of Canada's gift to Great Britain of $1 billion worth of war supplies.

Following the example set by Canadian Pacific Railways, many Canadian businesses fired employees of Japanese

Contempt for Danger

descent. Twelve hundred fishing boats owned by Japanese/Canadians were seized in British Columbia ports by the Canadian navy. Curfews were imposed on Japanese living in the vicinity of the Pacific coastline.

Four Japanese army divisions captured Kiska Island, an Alaskan atoll. Fearing imminent Japanese invasion of the North American mainland, all persons of Japanese descent residing within 35 miles of the Pacific coastline in Canada and the United States were ordered to register with their respective federal governments. In Canada twenty-one thousand residents of Japanese descent were thumb printed, issued identity cards, and relocated to eight inland detention centers – mostly abandoned mining camps. In June a Japanese submarine lobbed shells on Estevan Point, Vancouver Island. In retaliation Canadian planes bombed Japanese installations on Kiska Island. **Squadron Leader K.A. Boomer** downed a Japanese fighter off Alaska.

The Department of National Defense organized the *Canadian Rangers* in 1942. The Rangers were intended to be the *on the ground eyes and ears* of Canada's armed forces in the north. Approximately four thousand volunteered for training in this vital service. Armed with only rifles and knives Canadian Rangers criss-crossed Canada's Arctic on dogsled patrols with instructions to report anything unusual. The Canadian rangers celebrated their sixtieth birthday in 2002. The indestructible Lee-Enfield rifle continues to be the preferred weapon of the four-thousand-strong force as they skim over the Arctic on snowmobiles.

150

World Conflagration

From the beginning of 1942 German U-boats wreaked havoc along the Atlantic seaboard, concentrating most heavily on U.S. shipping. An adjunct to this heightened east coast activity was *the Battle of the St. Lawrence;* the huge saltwater basin separating Gaspe Peninsula from Newfoundland. The Battle of the St. Lawrence raged from May through mid October 1942. In the span of five months seven hundred lives were lost from the sinking of twenty-three ships by German U-boats.

In other sea action the Canadian Air Force lost seven planes attacking the *Scharnhorst* and *Gneisenau* as the German battle cruisers made good their escape from Brest, France to the North Sea. On this side of the Atlantic planes from *Eastern Command* sank two U-boats off the coast of Newfoundland.

28
Dieppe, France

In the summer of 1942 the French coastal community of *Dieppe* was the scene of a sea borne landing of disastrous proportion for its Canadian invaders.

Lieutenant General Andy McNaughton's *1st Canadian Army* had grown to five divisions and two armored brigades. The general's land forces had been training in the south of England since February 1940 and were anxious to see action. In contrast, Canada's navy and air force were in constant battle. Troops from other Commonwealth countries such as Australia, India, New Zealand and South Africa were fighting under British command in the Mediterranean Theater.

So when British Vice-Admiral Louis Mountbatten's Combined Operations Headquarters sought Canada's help in a raid on the Continent the British proposal was welcomed by McNaughton and Major General Harry Crerar, commander of 1st Canadian Corps. Code-named *Jubilee*, the concept involved a nine hour raid on Dieppe, a fortified town perched atop a cliff on the coast of France by a brigade level force of 5,000 to 6,000 men. Troops from *2nd Canadian Division* under Major General Hamilton Roberts were expected to overrun the town and move four miles inland to test the depth of German defenses. British commandos were to secure the Canadian flanks.

Dieppe, France

The Royal Navy transported 5,000 Canadian soldiers and 1,000 British commandos to Dieppe. A smattering of U.S. Army Rangers plus fifteen Free-French went along primarily as observers. Even before the raiding party got underway, both RAF Bomber Command and the Royal Navy opted not to provide heavy bombardment of Dieppe's coastal defenses. Some thought this support had already been assured. The RAF cited more pressing commitments, while the RN claimed they could not justify placing capital ships at risk. Nevertheless, the landings went ahead as scheduled - August 19, 1942. Swirling overhead was the largest air action Fighter Command had mounted since the Battle of Britain. Nine Canadian squadrons plus RAF Spitfires valiantly attempted to stem the seemingly endless strafing and bombing attacks by the Luftwaffe. The Germans downed 106 Allied fighters, losing only 48 of their own. Wehrmacht artillery mercilessly pounded the beachhead.

British landing craft conveying the Canadians were constructed of wood. Enemy bullets and shrapnel – even angle shots and glancing blows – tore through the wooden sides smashing into luckless troops huddled inside.

Charlie Merritt was born in Vancouver, British Columbia on November 10th 1908. He was a pupil at Lord Robert School in Vancouver before attending University High School in Victoria. Following his graduation from Royal Military College at Kingston, Ontario Charlie became an attorney-at-law. At age 21 he enlisted in the army reserve as an officer with the *Seaforth Highlanders Regiment*. When his regiment mobilized at the outbreak of war Merritt was promoted to lieutenant colonel

Contempt for Danger

and became a battalion commander with *2nd Canadian Infantry Division*'s *South Saskatchewan Regiment*.

Shortly after dawn on August 19, 1942 the *South Saskatchewan* and *Cameron Highlander* regiments landed on a stony tract of beach just west of Dieppe. Lieutenant Colonel Merritt's task was to capture and move across the Pourville Bridge over the River Scie into the outskirts of Dieppe. The enemy opened fire as the Saskatchewan Regiment approached the bridge.

The London Gazette said this of Lieutenant Colonel Merritt's Victoria Cross citation. *From the point of landing, his unit's advance had to be made across a bridge in Pourville which was swept by very heavy machinegun, mortar and artillery fire. The first parties were mostly destroyed and the bridge thickly covered by their bodies. A daring lead was required for the mission to succeed. Waving his helmet, Lieutenant Colonel Merritt rushed forward shouting, "Come on over! There's nothing to worry about here".*

He thus personally led the survivors of at least four parties in turn across the bridge. Quickly organizing these, he led them forward and when held up by enemy pillboxes he again headed rushes, which succeeded in clearing them. In one case he himself destroyed the occupants of the post by throwing grenades into it. After several of his runners became casualties, he himself kept contact with his different positions. Although twice wounded Lieutenant Colonel Merritt continued to direct the unit's operations with great vigor and determination and while organizing the withdrawal he stalked a sniper with a Bren gun and silenced him. He then coolly gave orders for the departure and announced his intention to hold off and 'get

154

Dieppe, France

even' with the enemy. When last seen he was collecting Bren and Tommy guns and preparing a defensive position which successfully covered the withdrawal from the beach. To this Commanding Officer's personal daring, the success of his unit's operations and the safe re-embarkation of a large portion of it were chiefly due.

In the absence of Allied naval and air bombardment, stiff German resistance soon rendered the sea borne raid a disaster. After 3,900 troops had been put ashore the landings were halted. Royal Navy landing craft withdrew to England taking 2,200 Canadians with them, half of whom were wounded. They left eight hundred Canadian dead on the beaches. The Germans took almost two thousand stranded soldiers prisoner, many suffering serious wounds, including Colonel Merritt.

Johnnie Foote was born in Madoc, Ontario May 5, 1904. He obtained his higher education at London's University of Western Ontario; at Queen's University in Kingston; and Montreal's McGill University. He entered the Presbyterian Ministry; later serving congregations in Fort Coulonge, Quebec and Port Hope, Ontario. Reverend Foote enlisted in the Canadian Chaplain Service in December 1939. Following his indoctrination Foote was given the rank of Honorary Captain, and posted to the *Hamilton Light Infantry Regiment, 4th Infantry Brigade, 2nd Canadian Infantry Division.* Subsequently Reverend Foote was appointed Regimental Chaplain.

Captain John Foote waded ashore with the Hamilton Light Infantry shortly after dawn under heavy fire. Chaplain Foote immediately attached himself to the Regimental Aid Post located in a slight depression on the beach. Actually it was

Contempt for Danger

little more than an indentation in the sand so shallow it only afforded cover to those lying prone.

For over eight hours the beach was swept with hostile fire. Time and again Chaplain Foote darted onto the open beach to inject morphine and administer first aid to the fallen. His gallant efforts saved many lives.

As the tide receded the Regimental Aid Post shifted to the shelter of a stranded landing craft. Captain Foote tirelessly carried wounded men across the exposed beach to the cover of the disabled landing craft. When they began to evacuate the wounded the Chaplain helped carry them from the Aid Post to the rescue boats. He declined several opportunities to be evacuated with the wounded. Instead, Chaplain Foote opted to suffer the same fate as the men he had ministered to for the past three years. He chose to become one of the 1,700 Canadians taken prisoner by the Germans.

His Victoria Cross citation said: *Honorary Captain Foote personally saved many lives by his efforts and his example inspired those around him. Those who observed him state that the calmness of this heroic officer as he walked about, collecting the wounded on the fire-swept beach will never be forgotten.*

Merritt and Foote remained prisoners of war until April 1945.

Upon his release from the army in 1945 Charles Merritt ran for public office and became a Member of Parliament, representing Vancouver-Burrard. Merritt resumed his Vancouver law practice after losing his parliamentary seat in the 1948 federal election. From 1951 through 1954 Lieutenant

Dieppe, France

Colonel Merritt served as commanding officer of the Seaforth Highlander Regiment Reserves. Charles Cecil Ingersoll Merritt died in his hometown of Vancouver July 12, 2000, at age 91.

Reverend Foote is the only member of the Canadian Chaplain Services ever to be awarded a Victoria Cross. Foote was promoted to the rank of major, and served with the Canadian Chaplain Service until 1948. After leaving the army Foote entered the provincial political arena. He was elected to the Ontario Legislature representing Durham County. He subsequently served as Ontario's Minister of Reform Institutions. John Weir Foote resided with his wife in Cobourg, Ontario until his death on May 2, 1988, three days shy of his 84th birthday.

John Hamilton Roberts was born in Pipestone, Manitoba in 1891. A graduate of Royal Military College in Kingston in 1914, Lieutenant Roberts shipped overseas with the Canadian Expeditionary Force as an artillery officer. He remained an artillery officer between the wars. Hamilton Roberts shipped overseas again in 1939. In June of the following year Colonel Roberts landed in France with the 1st Field Artillery Regiment. Roberts was credited with saving most of the regiment's heavy weapons when they were hastily evacuated from the Continent less than two weeks after arriving. Ham Roberts was promoted to brigadier general. Two years later, in 1942, Roberts was promoted to major general and given command of Canada's 2nd Infantry Division. Within four months of taking command Roberts led the Canadian assault on Dieppe. It was acknowledged following the post battle inquiry that since

Contempt for Danger

Roberts had no part in the planning of the Dieppe raid he was blameless for its failure. From then to the end of the war he served as a general officer overseeing Canadian reinforcement units. Hamilton Roberts died in 1962, at age 71.

British Admiral Louis Mountbatten awarded a medal to each U.S. Ranger who participated in the raid; Canadian troops, however, were not accorded similar honors. From the brutal tragedy of the *Raid on Dieppe* the Allies concluded that tanks and other tracked vehicles were useless on a pebble beach. After Dieppe no major Allied landings were attempted in such fragile landing craft, none were made against defendable port cities, none were attempted without first ensuring air superiority, nor were any conducted without the support of concentrated and sustainable air and naval bombardment.

29
Oran, Algeria

A national plebiscite in 1942 freed the Liberal government of its pledge not to seek conscription. While 63% of the national votes were in favor of the draft, 70% of Quebecers voted against the proposition. Although it had the public's vote of confidence, the government remained saddled with a caveat - conscripts could only be drafted to defend the homeland and were not to be sent overseas unless they volunteered for *General Service*.

In their letters home Canadian servicemen from all branches of service mentioned increasing friction between British and Canadian forces. For awhile Canadians had more money to spend than their British counterparts because of higher pay rates. However, the Canadian government eliminated this disparity by introducing a mandatory payroll deduction savings plan equivalent to the difference between British and Canadian pay scales. British officers were unhesitant in calling attention to perceived Canadian shortcomings in Royal Military Standards and etiquette; such as the way Canadians wore *the King's uniform*. Canadians were considered altogether too casual, and not properly respectful of their British superiors. Canadians on the other hand perceived English officers and non-commissioned officers as arrogant

Contempt for Danger

sticklers of regulation, often pompous and condescending in manner. Canadian resentment focused largely on the English rather than Irish, Scots and Welsh units with whom they apparently got along better.

In October 1942 the 80-ton RCMP patrol vessel *St. Roch* arrived in Sydney, Nova Scotia after successfully completing an arduous two-year voyage through the Arctic Ocean from the west coast. St. Roch was the first Canadian vessel to navigate the Northwest Passage.

The following month the *ALCAN Highway* was officially opened. The 1,600 mile military bush road connecting Dawson Creek, British Columbia with Fairbanks, Alaska was built primarily by the U.S. Army Corps of Engineers despite the fact that three quarters of the road was located in Canada.

During 1942 the Canadian Navy reported the loss of the destroyer *Ottawa*, two corvettes - *Spikenard* and *Charlottetown* - as well as the armed-yacht *Raccoon*. In November, *Convoy ONS-54* under escort by the Canadian Navy lost 14 of its 46 ships.

In the Mediterranean Theater Rommel's *Afrika Corps*, after conquering the British fortress at Tobruk, was now threatening Cairo. Yet by the fall of 1942 the fortunes of war began to swing in favor of the Allies. In North Africa General Bernard Montgomery's British 8th Army – *the Desert Rats* - inflicted heavy losses on the Afrika Corps at El Alamein. A strong Anglo/American task force led by U.S. *General Dwight Eisenhower* landed in Northwest Africa and plowed forcefully eastward.

160

Oran, Algeria

Although Canadian forces did not participate in the North African Campaign as an organized group, individual Canadians did. In fact a Canadian was awarded a Victoria Cross there.

Fred Peters was born in Charlottetown, Prince Edward Island September 17, 1889. Fred's father was the Attorney General as well as the first Liberal Premier of the province. Fred attended St. Peter's Private School. He also attended school in Victoria, British Columbia. Subsequently Fred became a cadet at the Royal Naval School in England where he graduated as a midshipman.

Three years later Midshipman Fred Peters was commissioned a sub-lieutenant in the Royal Navy. During World War I, Lieutenant Peters was awarded the *Distinguished Service Order*, a first for a Canadian, as well as a *Distinguished Service Cross*. Over the next twenty years Peters was promoted to naval captain, equivalent in rank to an army colonel.

On May 18, 1943 the London Gazette reported: *Captain Peters was in the suicide-charge by two little cutters at Oran. Walney and Harland were two ex-American coastguard cutters which were lost in a gallant attempt to force the boom defenses in the harbor of Oran during the landings on the North African coast. Captain Peters led his force through the boom in the face of point-blank fire from shore batteries, a destroyer and a cruiser - a feat which was described as one of the great episodes of naval history. The Walney reached the jetty disabled and ablaze, and went down with her colors flying. Blinded in one eye, Captain Peters was the only survivor of the seventeen men on the bridge of the Walney. He was taken prisoner but was later*

Contempt for Danger

released when Oran was captured. On being liberated from the jail, he was carried through the streets where the citizens hailed him with flowers.

On November 13, 1942 just five days following his release from the Oran jail, Captain Peters was killed when the Sunderland aircraft returning him from Algeria to Britain crashed off the coast of England. Frederick Thornton Peters was 54 years of age at the time of his death.

30
On the Offensive

6th Canadian Bomber Group went operational January 1st, 1943. Canada's Air Force now comprised 67 squadrons; 31 overseas plus another 36 back home. Canadian aircrew assigned to Bomber Command had begun to fly the new four-engine heavy bombers - Lancasters and Halifaxes.

Hundreds of *Avro Lancaster* bombers were built in Canada. Twelve Canadian squadrons were eventually equipped with them. Armed with nine .30 caliber machine guns, the all-metal stressed-skin Lancaster could lug seven tons of bombs at 275 miles per hour at heights of up to 25,000 feet. The big plane had a crew of seven – pilot, flight engineer, navigator, radio operator, bomb-aimer/front gunner, mid upper gunner, and tail gunner.

Another popular Canadian heavy bomber was the *Handley Page Halifax*. Its four engines could haul a seven ton bomb load at 285 miles per hour at heights of 24,000 feet. Similar to the Lancaster, the Halifax was also armed with nine .30 caliber machine guns.

In eastern Europe the tides of war began to shift. Soviet forces employed a pincer strategy to smash through Axis lines north and south of Stalingrad, successfully engulfing a huge German army. On January 30th 1943 Field Marshal von Paulus,

Contempt for Danger

commander of the German Sixth Army surrendered to Soviet forces at Stalingrad. In less than ninety days 300,000 Germans had been killed, starved to death or had succumbed to the cold. Another 100,000 Germans were marched into Soviet captivity.

In the spring of 1943 thirty Canadian airmen flew with RAF squadrons in the now famous dam-buster raids over the Ruhr Valley. Closer to home Canadian *Rear Admiral Leonard Murray* was promoted to commander-in-chief Northwest Atlantic. Murray's headquarters shifted from St. John's to Halifax.

Axis forces were squeezed out of North Africa in May when the United States Army charging from the west linked-up with a massive British push from the east. At Kursk, Soviet forces severely mauled the Wehrmacht in the greatest tank battle in history.

Lieutenant General Andy McNaughton had been at loggerheads with the British high command for months. McNaughton believed Canada's expeditionary force should fight as a cohesive unit, the British thought otherwise. Great Britain still very much regarded Canada as a *colonial power*, not a full ally, and London insisted that *Colonials* be integrated with Britain's own armed forces. For months neither side budged. Canadian land forces had been excluded from the North African campaign and were being ignored in the planning for the invasion of Italy.

McNaughton was convinced Britain was prepared to relegate indefinitely Canada's entire expeditionary force to reserve status. This might well have been the case had Ottawa not intervened by appealing directly to British Prime Minister

On the Offensive

Winston Churchill. It was decided Canada could field a fighting division in the upcoming invasion of Sicily provided it was placed under command of British 8th Army.

In late June nine heavily laden ships hoisted anchor and moved down the Clyde Estuary. The convoy maneuvered past the anti-submarine boom at Glasgow and on into the open sea. Aboard the drab gray liners were 27,000 troops of 1st Canadian Infantry Division. There were a few alerts but no attacks during the twelve day voyage. In the Mediterranean they met up with a vast flotilla of warships, liners, freighters and landing craft.

At 0500 on July 10 American, British and Canadian forces stormed the beaches of southeastern Sicily. Thirty-nine year old Canadian *Major General Guy Simonds* led *1st Division* ashore under air cover of Spitfires from *# 417 Canadian Fighter Squadron*. Canadian troops landed on the Pachino peninsula. They were on the left flank of General Montgomery's British 8th Army and the right flank of General George Patton's U.S. 7th Army. Eighth Army was to move north over the mountains directly to Messina. Seventh Army would take Palermo in the northwest before cutting east to link-up with the British at Messina.

The day was hot, about 95 degrees Fahrenheit, not a cloud in the sky. Canadian landings went unopposed. That night, however, the Luftwaffe bombed and strafed their landing site. Ironically most injuries were caused by falling shrapnel from Allied anti-aircraft guns.

The main thrust of the British advance followed the highway to Mount Etna, pausing only when encountering

165

Contempt for Danger

enemy resistance. Other British units moved up the coastline. On the left flank Canadian troops had to plod across mountainous terrain. The land was hot, dry and enveloped in powdery dust. Italian forces put up little resistance and the Canadians were able to pretty much proceed at the pace of the mule trains hauling their supplies. Resistance stiffened when they arrived at the German defense line near the town of Leonforte in the foothills of Mount Etna, an active fiery volcano.

Simonds' troops scaled a one thousand foot cliff on July 22 to capture a German-held fort at Assoro. Six days later they took Agira, the scene of Canada's bloodiest battle in Sicily. Victorious Canadian troops and Agira townspeople were treated to musical passages by Vancouver's Seaforth Highlanders military band. By August 17 Allied forces had conquered the entire island.

On July 25 Benito Mussolini, fascist leader of Italy for two decades, was deposed. When newly appointed Italian Prime Minister Badoglio signed an armistice with the Allies, German troops quickly occupied Italian cities and took over defensive positions manned by their former Axis partner.

Trans Canada Airlines (TCA) began regular flights to England using modified Lancaster bombers to carry paying passengers. The military/civilian aircraft completed the 3,000-mile flight from Montreal to Britain in 13 hours. In August, Prime Minister Mackenzie King hosted a war strategy conference in Quebec City convened by British Prime Minister Winston Churchill and U.S. President Franklin Roosevelt.

On the Offensive

On September 3rd Allied forces landed at the toe of Italy. *1st Canadian Division* hit the beaches at Reggio. Moving on they overcame fierce German resistance in the capture of Campobasso.

Paul Triquet was born in Cabano, Quebec April 2, 1910. While attending Cabano Academy High School, Paul joined the Army Cadet Corps. In 1927 he enlisted in the regular army as a private with the *22nd Regiment*. During the six years he was stationed in Quebec City Paul Triquet attended night school to improve his education.

In 1943 Captain Triquet was a company commander with the *22nd Regiment, 3rd Brigade* serving on the Italian front. *1st Canadian Infantry Division* had fought its way through Sicily, and up the Italian boot to Ortona. Just ahead lay a key road junction on the main Ortona-Orsogna highway, Casa Berardi. German tanks and infantry were dug-in at Casa Berardi as well as the gully leading up to the hamlet.

On December 14th Captain Triquet's company, supported by a squadron of tanks was ordered to cross the gully and secure Casa Berardi. As the Canadians moved into the valley they were subjected to heavy machinegun and mortar fire. The company sustained 50% casualties, including all of Triquet's officers. Captain Triquet went round to all the survivors, reorganizing them and offering his men encouragement. When enemy troops were seen infiltrating from all sides Captain Triquet shouted: "There are enemy in front of us, behind us and on our flanks. There is only one safe place – and that's our objective." The company commander dashed forward and his

Contempt for Danger

men followed. The Germany line crumbled. In the process the Canadian force destroyed four tanks and silenced several enemy machinegun posts. Yet they still had to take Berardi.

Captain Triquet and his company in close cooperation with a squadron of tanks forced their way into the outskirts of Casa Berardi. Captain Triquet immediately devised a defensive perimeter around his tanks with the remainder of the company; two sergeants and fifteen men.

The Germans counterattacked with tanks and infantry. Ignoring the heavy fire, Triquet darted amongst his men, encouraging them and directing their defense, personally killing several of the enemy. The Germans withdrew. For the rest of the day and throughout the night Captain Triquet and his small force held out against renewed attacks until the rest of the battalion arrived and they were relieved.

The French Government awarded Captain Triquet the *Chevalier de Legion d' Honneur*. For that same action Captain Triquet was also awarded the Victoria Cross.

Captain Triquet's Victoria Cross citation was reported in the London Gazette on March 6, 1944. *Throughout the whole of this engagement Captain Triquet showed the most magnificent courage and cheerfulness under heavy fire. Wherever the action was the hottest he was often seen shouting encouragement to his men and organizing the defense. His utter disregard of danger, his cheerfulness and tireless devotion to duty were a constant source of inspiration to them. His tactical skill and leadership enabled them, although reduced by casualties to a mere handful, to continue their advance against bitter resistance and to hold their gains against determined*

On the Offensive

counterattacks. It was due to him that Casa Berardi was captured and the way opened for the attack on the vital road junction.

In 1947 Paul Triquet retired from the Canadian Army to become a district sales manager for a Quebec forest products company. During the Korean War he returned to the army and was appointed Commanding Officer of a reserve regiment at Levis, Quebec. In 1954 Paul Triquet was promoted to Colonel and placed in command of the 8th Militia Group. After retiring from military service a second time, Triquet divided his time between Florida and Quebec. Colonel Paul Triquet died August 8, 1980 at 70 years-of-age.

A week prior to Christmas 1943 *1st Canadian Division* crossed the Moro River in a bloody campaign taking them all the way to the port city of Ortona. Capturing Ortona involved intense door-to-door fighting against German paratroopers and tanks.

Canadian forces eventually prevailed at Ortona after suffering almost 2,400 casualties. By now 1st Division needed help; specifically a tank army. When *Canadian 5th Armored* was shipped from England to bolster 1st Infantry Division in Italy, General Andy McNaughton became so frustrated with the gradual dilution of his authority in England he relinquished command of 1st Canadian Army and returned home to Canada.

Andrew George Latta McNaughton was born in Moosomin, Saskatchewan in 1887. He majored in physics and engineering, graduating with a masters degree from McGill University in 1912. Lieutenant McNaughton shipped overseas with 4th

Contempt for Danger

Artillery Battery, Canadian Expeditionary Force in 1914. By war's end he was in charge of the Canadian artillery corps. In the 1930s McNaugton served as Chief of the General Staff until he took a leave of absence to head the National Research Council of Canada, a position he held from 1935 through 1939. He returned to the army at the outbreak of war to assume command of 1st Canadian Infantry Division. His responsibilities grew as the Canadian Expeditionary Force expanded in size; first as a corps in 1940 and as an Army two years later. General MacNaughton antagonized too many senior British Army officials by his insistence his army fight as a cohesive unit, and that Britain regard Canada as a full ally allowing it to become involved in strategic war planning. He never won his case. In frustration General McNaughton resigned his command in 1943 and returned to Canada. In 1944 he was appointed Minister of Defense by Prime Minister MacKenzie King. Following the war McNaughton headed the Canadian Atomic Energy Control Commission, representing Canada at the United Nations 1948-1949. From 1950-1959 he was president of the Canadian section of the International Atomic Energy Commission. Andrew McNaughton died at Montebello, Quebec in 1966. He was 79.

Had Canada's navy, army, and air force been allowed to fight as cohesive units Canada may have been accorded a say in issues of strategic significance. However, Britain would not consider it.

Not only was Canada excluded from top political and military planning, few beyond Canada were aware of the

On the Offensive

immensity of Canada's contribution to the war effort. This was not surprising considering that Canada's forces were divided and its fighting contingents subordinated to British Command. As a result little was reported in international media concerning Canada's accomplishments. War dispatches referring to Canadian units typically cited '...RAF....did this' or '...elements of the British Army...did that'. The Canadian armed forces publication *Maple Leaf* did at least help Canada's military keep informed of relevant Canadian news. Maple Leaf was similar in concept to its American counterpart *Stars and Stripes*.

In November Prime Minister King appointed *Leighton McCarthy* as *Canada's first ambassador to the United States*. In return the United States upgraded its representation in Ottawa to full ambassador status. The United States was the first nation to accord Canada the international recognition it had long desired.

In 1943 the Canadian Navy reported the loss of destroyer *St. Croix*, corvettes *Louisburg* and *Weyburn* and, on October 21, the minesweeper *Chedabucto*. However, the Allies were now winning the battle of the Atlantic. In 1942 U-boats sank an average of 650,000 tons of Allied shipping each month; in 1943 the average had shrunk to 18,000 tons per month. In one seven week stint Canadian planes sank four U-Boats.

31
Objective Maungdaw, Burma

In January 1944 the Soviet Army broke the 2-1/2 year German stranglehold on Leningrad. Years later the great city would revert to its original name *Saint Petersburg*.

Charlie Hoey was born in Duncan, British Columbia March 29, 1914. Duncan lies north of Victoria on Vancouver Island. Charlie attended Duncan Grammar School and Duncan High School. In 1933, at the height of the *Great Depression*, Charles Hoey went to England in hopes of making a career in the British Army. After enlisting in the West Kent Regiment he won a cadetship to Royal Military College at Sandhurst. Hoey graduated from Sandhurst in December 1936. After returning from leave in his hometown of Duncan, Hoey was assigned to 2nd *Battalion*, Lincolnshire *Regiment*. In September 1937 Hoey transferred to the regiment's *1st Battalion* stationed in India.

In 1942 the regiment relocated from India to Burma. In July of 1943 Major Hoey won a *Military Cross* for outstanding action in a raid on a Japanese position.

Thirteen months later, on February 16, 1944 Major Hoey's company was part of a larger force ordered to capture a Japanese position near Maungdaw. A night march through enemy held territory attracted heavy machinegun and rifle fire as the force drew closer to its objective.

Objective Maungdaw, Burma

In the process of leading his company toward its objective Major Hoey was wounded three times – once in the head, twice in the leg. Still he forced himself forward. Hoey grabbed a Bren gun from one of his men and, firing from the hip, led his men right up to the objective. His troopers had difficulty keeping pace with their wounded commander with the result the major reached the enemy stronghold first. Hoey didn't hesitate. He killed the occupants before being fatally hit by a sniper's bullet.

His Victoria Cross citation reads: *Major Hoey's outstanding gallantry and leadership, his total disregard of personal safety and his grim determination to reach the objective resulted in the capture of this vital position.* Major Charles Ferguson Hoey was a month shy of his 30th birthday when cut down by enemy fire at Maungdaw, Burma.

32
Melfa River, Italy

On the Italian front in the spring of 1944 tanks of Canada's *5th Armored* participated in a major initiative near Casino which led to the Germans being forced to abandon their defenses. At Pontecorvo in the Liri Valley *1st Infantry* and *5th Armored* smashed through the Hitler Line - a blockade of minefields, trenches, bunkers and infantry.

Johnnie Mahony was born in New Westminster, British Columbia June 30, 1911. After graduating from Duke of Connaught High School, John Mahony became a reporter for the Vancouver Province. As a militia officer when World War II broke out Mahony was one of the first in his unit to enlist in the regular army.

Major John Mahony commanded *Company A, Westminster Regiment, 5th Canadian Armored Division* based in Italy. On May 24, 1944 his Regiment was ordered to establish a bridgehead across the Melfa River. On the east bank of the Melfa the Germans had a strong force of weapons and infantry. Major Mahony personally positioned his platoons on the west bank preparatory to crossing the river. Mahony was with his lead platoon when it made the crossing. The Melfa River crossing was achieved in full view of enemy machinegun posts. *Company A* established a small bridgehead on ground so hard that only shallow weapons-pits could be dug. Reinforcements

174

Melfa River, Italy

wouldn't arrive until 10:30 that night when other companies and supporting weapons could cross the river under cover of darkness.

Enemy troops kept *Company A* boxed in on three sides for five hours. The Germans were equipped with tanks, two 88 mm self-propelled guns, 4 anti-aircraft guns, Spandau machineguns, infantry and a mortar company.

Even as the Canadians were establishing their bridgehead, the enemy counter-attacked with infantry supported by tanks and self-propelled guns. *Company A* fought with mortars, grenades and PIATs. PIAT, the military acronym for *Projector, Infantry, Anti-Tank,* is a cross between an anti-tank rifle and a U.S. Army bazooka. Mahony personally organized the company's defensive position, and directed the fire of the PIATs. *Company A* repelled the counterattack yet sustained 50% casualties, including all but one platoon officer.

Scarcely an hour later enemy tanks and infantry mounted a second counterattack against the remaining sixty soldiers of *Company A.* Major Mahony scurried from section to section offering words of encouragement to his men despite having been wounded in the head and twice in the leg.

At one stage of the battle when a section was pinned down by intense machinegun fire Mahony crawled to their position. By hurling smoke grenades he succeeded in extricating the section from its precarious position at the loss of only one man. After the Canadians put three self-propelled guns and a Panther tank out of action the German counterattack fizzled out.

Contempt for Danger

Although Mahony was in extreme pain he refused medical aid and continued to direct the defense of the bridgehead. Only after reinforcements arrived would the major allow his wounds to be dressed. Even then he insisted on remaining with his company, refusing to be evacuated.

Major John Mahony's Victoria Cross citation as reported in the London Gazette said: *The forming and holding of a bridgehead across the river was vital to the whole Canadian Corps action, and failure would have meant delay, a repetition of the attack, probably involving heavy losses in men, materiel and time, and would have given the enemy a breathing space which might have broken the impetus of the Corps' advance.*

The Gazette added: *Major Mahony, knowing this, never allowed the thought of failure or withdrawal to enter his mind, and infused his spirit and determination into all his men. The enemy perceived this officer was the soul of the defense and consequently fired at him constantly with all weapons, from rifle to 88 mm guns. Major Mahony completely ignored the enemy fire and with great courage and absolute disregard for personal danger commanded his company with such great confidence, energy and skill that the enemy's efforts to destroy the bridgehead were all defeated. The great courage shown by Major Mahony in this action will forever be an inspiration to his Regiment and to the Canadian Army.*

Mahony held a succession of positions with the army following the war. In 1954 Lieutenant Colonel Mahony served as Canadian Army Liaison Officer at the Canadian Embassy in Washington, D.C. He retired from the army in 1962. John Keefer Mahony died December 16, 1990 at age 79.

33
Devil's Brigade

Devil's Brigade was the sobriquet bestowed on First Special Service Force (FSSF) by baffled Germans at Anzio Beachhead in southwest Italy. On January 22nd 1944 U.S. forces landed at Anzio intending to leapfrog the seemingly impenetrable German winter line spanning Italy to the south. Although American forces quickly established a fifteen mile beachhead they were unable to break free of their limited toehold. The Wehrmacht held the high ground and were heavily dug-in. The FSSF - a specially trained brigade comprising American and Canadian volunteers - went ashore at Anzio to assist beleaguered American assault troops on the beachhead.

The FSSF routinely sent small reconnaissance teams out on night raids to estimate enemy strength and to generally create havoc. When they came across sleeping enemy soldiers their tendency was to slit the throat of a sole German, allowing the others to remain asleep. Then they would stick a message written in German on the dead body: *The Worst Is Yet to Come*, or *Black Devil's Were Here.* On other occasions the night stalkers didn't kill anyone. Instead they simply stole the Germans' weapons, leaving behind one of their *calling-card-stickers*. It wasn't long before intercepted German dispatches from Anzio were making reference to a mysterious *Devil's Brigade.*

Contempt for Danger

Montreal born **Major Tom Gilday** was a battalion commander with the First Special Service Force. For ten years Gilday had been an officer with the Canadian Grenadier Guards, later to become Canadian 4th Armored Brigade. In the summer of 1942 Captain Gilday was selected as a founding member of an elite international force. To avoid confusion with Britain's Royal Army Commandos or U.S. Army Rangers, the newly created fighting unit was given the innocuous name of *First Special Service Force*. Half the original troop complement was drawn from the Canadian Army, half from the U.S. Army - all volunteers. Gilday was promoted to major and given command of the brigade's newly created 1st Battalion, 3rd Regiment. The FSSF was outfitted in U.S. Army uniforms and gear.

Trained in demolitions, the FSSF undertook winter training at Fort Harrison near Helena, Montana. They completed parachute training at Fort Benning, Georgia, rock climbing in Vermont, and amphibious training in Virginia. Ostensibly they were being groomed to destroy German heavy-water plants in Norway. As it developed, however, their first mission was to liberate Kiska, Alaska. In early 1942 sixty thousand Japanese troops had taken possession of the American atoll west of mainland Alaska. In August of 1943 the brigade landed on a Kiska beach in heavy fog. The Allied invaders crossed the island preparatory to attacking the enemy from the rear. They were astonished to discover that the Japanese had completely evacuated the atoll. Hot cooking stoves in deserted mess halls indicated the last of the Japanese occupiers had only recently

Devil's Brigade

departed. The disappointed FSSF invaders were transported back to Virginia where they remained for three months. In November they shipped out to Casablanca, Morocco.

The first battle the FSSF fought was at Monte la Difensa on the Italian mainland where German troops controlled a string of mountains south of Rome spanning the entire width of Italy. Monte la Difensa was the cornerstone of the enemy's defense line. British troops had tried unsuccessfully to take the mountain, so had American forces. On a dark night FSSF units slipped undetected through German lines, stealthily making their way north to the base of the mountain's reverse slope. They hid throughout the day and the following evening, during a heavy rainstorm, scaled the 350 foot face of Monte la Difensa's reverse slope. Thousands of FSSF troops including Major Gilday hauled their equipment up the slippery, craggy rock-face.

The dawn assault from the rear took the Germans completely by surprise. Nevertheless the enemy mounted a spirited defense and it took four hours of bloody fighting before the FSSF achieved victory.

Following their baptism of fire the Canadian/US mountain troops fought briefly on the Casino front before shifting to toward the east coast. Again they scaled a mountain to catch its German defenders by surprise. This successful FSSF maneuver relieved pressure the Wehrmacht had begun to apply against a fresh Canadian assault just getting underway north of Ortona.

Their next assignment was the fifteen mile pocket beachhead established at Anzio by the U.S. Army in January.

179

Contempt for Danger

For ninety-nine days Special Force units sustained casualties from relentless enemy artillery fire. When finally relieved, the FSSF were placed in the vanguard of the U.S. 5th Army's march on the Italian capital.

The joint Canadian/American battle force entered Rome on June 4th. Their speedy advance enabled them to secure the Saint Marguerite Bridge leading to Vatican City before it could be blown-up by the Germans. Rome was liberated the next day. In an expression of gratitude for Rome's deliverance, elements of the FSSF were granted an audience with Pope Pius XII. Other Allied forces had now entered Rome and members of the Royal Canadian Regiment Corps of Drums provided musical accompaniment at the Vatican reception.

On August 15th the FSSF landed from inflatable boats on the south coast of France near Marseilles. This invasion marked the beginning of the final actions of the now famous international fighting unit. By December of 1944 the need for a specially trained international brigade was considered redundant and the unit was disbanded.

After Anzio Tom Gilday was promoted to lieutenant colonel, sent to Belgium and given command of the Regina Rifles Infantry Regiment during the fighting for the Scheldt Estuary. In December Lieutenant Colonel Gilday became a staff officer at First Canadian Army headquarters. After the war Gilday established his own insurance-adjusting business in Sudbury, Ontario. Upon his retirement in 1970 Tom and his wife relocated to Toronto. The heroic Devil's Brigade battalion commander died in Toronto in June 2001 at age 96.

180

34
Juno Beach

Hitting the silk at five minutes past midnight meant the advance elements of 1st Canadian Parachute Battalion were the first Allied soldiers to land in France on D-Day the 6th of June 1944.

1st Canadian Parachute Battalion was born July 1942 amidst fears of imminent invasion of North America by German or Japanese forces. Conceived as a rapid deployment unit for home defense *1st Para* was initially a small force of about six hundred. The newly created battle unit completed four months intensive training at Fort Benning, Georgia. Subsequent Canadian parachutists graduated from the Canadian Army's new parachute training facility constructed at Camp Shilo, Manitoba. Shilo was closely patterned along U.S. Army Airborne training practices.

1st Para constituted a headquarters company plus three rifle companies under command of Lieutenant Colonel George Bradbrook, a former Saskatoon Light Infantry regimental officer. When the battalion shipped out from Camp Shilo in 1943 it linked up with the British Army's 6th Airborne Division then training in the south of England. Over the next eleven months 1st Para practiced airborne maneuvers, and honed its weapons-handling and demolitions skills.

Contempt for Danger

In the evening of June 5th one hundred and ten men from C Company, designated as the advance unit, were whisked off in Albemarle bombers. An hour later A, B and Headquarters Companies embarked in twenty-five Douglas Dakota transports from another airfield; taking off at forty-five second intervals. 1st Para's objective was the capture of two bridges, destruction of several others, and nullifying enemy gun installations in the vicinity of Merville, France.

Five hundred and forty-three troops of 1st Canadian Parachute Battalion dropped into France in the early hours of June 6th. Twenty-seven officers and five hundred and sixteen enlisted men achieved their objectives at a cost of 113 casualties. Elsewhere in Normandy thousands of British and American paratroopers augmented by glider formations pursued similar targets. As dawn broke American, British and Canadian infantry divisions began storming the beaches of Normandy in the greatest sea-borne landing in history.

D-Day was the execution date of *Operation Overlord*, code name for the Allied invasion of Occupied France. The target – Normandy's beaches extending west from Le Havre toward the Cherbourg Peninsula. The beachhead was organized into five coded sectors: Utah, Omaha, Gold, Juno and Sword. American forces focused on the western beaches of Utah and Omaha. To the east British troops tackled Gold and Sword. Inserted between Gold and Sword was Juno Beach where Canada's troops landed.

Fourteen thousand Canadian troops, comprising ten battalions of infantry from *3rd Division* plus three regiments

Juno Beach

from *2nd Armored Brigade,* under command of Canadian Major General Rod Keller landed at *Juno Beach.* General Keller's target was a five mile stretch of sandy beach including the coastal communities of Courseulles, Bernieres and St. Aubin.

Rodney Frederick Leopold Keller was born in Tetbury, England in 1900. He immigrated to Canada at a young age. Upon graduation from Royal Military College he joined the Princess Patricia's Canadian Light Infantry. He was a major when he shipped overseas with his regiment. In 1941 he was promoted to brigadier general and assumed command of 1st Infantry Brigade. The following year he was elevated to major general and given command of 3rd Infantry Division whom he led in the invasion of Normandy. Keller was wounded by friendly fire on August 8th and never returned to field command. Ironically, Rod Keller died while visiting Normandy ten years later in 1954.

To help withstand the Allied invasion of Fortress Europe the Germans heavily mined the coastal waters. In addition, steel girder configurations called Hedgehogs were anchored below high-tide level in anticipation of impaling landing craft before they reached shore. Once ashore the Canadians had to contend with barbed wire, mines, concrete bunkers, pill boxes and extensive networks of tunnels.

With the United States assuming responsibility for the design of troop landing craft following the Dieppe raid Allied forces at Normandy had three basic steel hull assault craft at their disposal: LSTs (Landing Ship Tank) capable of transporting 20 tanks, LCIs (Landing Ship Infantry) toting

Contempt for Danger

two hundred fully equipped infantrymen, plus fleets of LCVPs.

Landing Craft Vehicles and Personnel, or LCVPs, were small assault craft - 36 feet long, 10-1/2 feet wide - capable of carrying three dozen fully equipped infantrymen onto the beaches. The dogged craft were also known as *Higgins Boats* in deference to Irish/American shipbuilder Andrew Higgins. Higgins Industries of New Orleans, Louisiana constructed thousands of the amphibious assault craft used by the Allies in the European and Pacific theaters.

Off the Normandy coast capital ships – battleships and cruisers – of the United States, Britain and France laid down a heavy barrage beyond the beaches. The big ships were supported by an armada of smaller ships from several nations: Australia, Britain, Canada, France, Greece, the Netherlands, Poland and the United States. Nine thousand seven hundred Canadian sailors manned the one hundred and eight Canadian vessels - destroyers, minesweepers, troop transports, motor torpedo boats and landing craft - plying the busy waters off Normandy.

Canada supplied two troop ships – the Prince David and Prince Henry – former Canada Steamship passenger liners. Green painted maple leaf emblems adorned the funnels of the otherwise camouflaged armed merchant ships. The huge transports carried troops and supplies to Normandy and wounded back to England. Large troop ships anchored about six miles offshore and relied on assault craft to provide ferry service to and from shore.

184

Juno Beach

Two flotillas of eight Canadian MTBs (motor torpedo boats) guarded the watery flanks of the invasion forces against German surface attack. Three U.S. built Packard in-board engines powered each seventy foot long Canadian MTB capable of speeds of up to fifty miles per hour.

Canadian forces utilized a variety of new and innovative planes, tanks, and ground transport in the invasion.

Airborne troops parachuted from twin-engine *Dakota* cargo planes known as the DC-3 by commercial airlines. The all-metal stressed-skin Dakota was manufactured by the Douglas Aircraft Company. When converted to military usage an aircrew of three flew Dakotas capable of toting 4-1/2 ton payloads at speeds of up to 230 miles per hour as high as 23,000 feet. Canadian crews flew Dakotas extensively in Burma as well as Europe. From D-Day through the end of the war the majority of airborne drops were from Dakota aircraft.

Four Canadian squadrons flew the new *Hawker Typhoon* fighter-bomber. With a speed of more than 400 miles per hour the Typhoon was one of the fastest planes in the world. It was armed with four .20 mm cannon and could carry a ton of bombs or eight rockets. Typhoons used in close air support of infantry could be called upon to take-out roadblocks, bunkers, enemy tanks as well as other obstructions.

Until mid 1942 Canadian armored units fought with British designed Churchill tanks. After Dieppe the U.S. designed *M4 General Sherman* became Canadian Armored's main battle tank. The 30-ton Sherman was a medium tank capable of attaining 30 miles per hour with a range of 150 miles between fuelings.

185

Contempt for Danger

Canadian Shermans were typically armed with a 70 mm gun and two machineguns. They had a crew of five - commander, driver, assistant driver, gunner, and loader.

Speedy ground reconnaissance was achieved with the British designed *Bren Carrier*. The versatile lightly armored tracked vehicle was also used as a weapons transporter and troop carrier. When used as a fighting vehicle the Bren carrier could be rigged with a machine gun, mortar, anti-tank gun, or flamethrower.

Another highly versatile rugged vehicle was the *Jeep*. This U.S. designed quarter-ton four-wheel drive utility vehicle was used by all Allied forces. Manufactured by Willys Overland Company, and later by the Ford Motor Company, the jeep could travel at 55 miles per hour. It was used for all forms of quick transport including stretcher bearing.

Canadians boarded designated naval craft in Portsmouth, England the morning of June 4th in anticipation of landing in France the following day. However, bad weather delayed the landings by twenty-four hours. By the time landing ramps dropped two days later most troops had been violently seasick at some point during their choppy voyage. They were understandably anxious to vacate the confined quarters of the vomit sloshing landing craft yet as soon as the ramp dropped they were peppered with machinegun fire and shrapnel. Most who made it from the craft in the early morning of Tuesday, June 6, 1944 stepped into water above their waists. One company of Regina infantry suffered ninety-two casualties out of its 120 man complement.

Juno Beach

Overhead, Canadian fighters escorting 230 Canadian bombers formed part of a huge Allied air armada. In all, 30,000 Canadians participated in the Normandy invasion. Before D-day was over, Canadian assault forces sustained over 1,100 casualties. The beaches claimed the greatest toll: 366 dead or dying, 548 wounded, another 110 missing. Canadian airborne troops landing behind enemy lines suffered nineteen killed, ten wounded and eighty-four missing in action.

Keller's troops fought the Wehrmacht's 716th and 21st Panzer Divisions. His command advanced farther inland on D-Day than any other Allied unit. Days later they were caught up in battle with the 12th SS Hitlerjugend Division.

Canadian army recruiting practice encouraged friends and relatives to join the same unit with promises of being able to train and fight together. Viewed as a morale booster by the War Department the fate of community-raised battle units often heightened the anguish suffered by next of kin. Mr and Mrs Westlake, for instance, lost three sons in the Battle for Normandy. Son George Westlake fell on June 7, sons Albert and Thomas four days later. The Westlake boys are buried at the Canadian War Cemetery at Beny-Sur-Mer near Caen, along with 2,035 other Canadians, including nine pairs of brothers.

To this day the Allied invasion of Normandy remains the largest sea borne landing in history. Within the first twenty-four hours 75,000 British Commonwealth troops plus 58,000 American forces were put ashore, along with a wide variety of tanks, artillery and heavy equipment. What distinguished Canadian forces from those of other nations in

Contempt for Danger

the Battle for Normandy was the fact that all Canadians were volunteers.

Before the Normandy campaign ended eighty-five days later, Canadian forces sustained 18,444 casualties, including 5,021 killed in action.

35
Air Force Blue

Andy Mynarski was born in Winnipeg, Manitoba October 14, 1916. Andy attended King Edward and Isaac Newton Elementary Schools, as well as St. John's Technical School. To help support his family following his father's death Andy took a job as a leather worker. In November 1941, 25-year-old Andy Mynarski joined the Canadian Air Force, training at Calgary and Edmonton, Alberta as well as at MacDonald, Manitoba. In December 1942 Mynarski shipped overseas.

On June 12, 1944 Pilot Officer Mynarski was filling in as mid-upper gunner on a bomber destined to attack Cambrai when enemy night-fighters attacked their Lancaster from below and astern. Both port engines of the Canadian plane failed. Fire erupted in the fuselage between the mid-upper turret and the tail. The left wing caught fire, producing flames so fierce the captain ordered his crew to bail-out.

As Mynarski left his turret and struggled toward the escape hatch he noticed the rear gunner had not left his station. Mynarski's parachute and clothes from the waist up caught fire as he edged through the flames to reach the rear turret. His attempts to release the trapped gunner proved futile. The hydraulic gear had been put out of action when the port engines failed, and the manual release was broken. The

Contempt for Danger

situation appeared hopeless and the rear gunner waved Mynarski off. Reluctantly Mynarski crawled back to the escape hatch.

As a final gesture to his trapped buddy, Pilot Officer Andrew Mynarski turned toward the rear gunner, stood at attention in his flaming clothes and parachute, saluted, and stepped through the escape hatch. French witnesses on the ground watched the agonizing descent of an Allied airman whose flaming clothes and parachute lit up the sky. He was still alive when the French found him, but the life of the severely burned officer could not be saved.

The rear gunner had a miraculous escape when the Lancaster crashed. He subsequently testified that had Pilot Officer Mynarski not attempted to save his life, Mynarski could have exited the aircraft safely.

The London Gazette reported Pilot Officer Andrew Mynarski's Victoria Cross citation on October 11, 1946. *Pilot Officer Mynarski must have been fully aware that in trying to free the rear gunner he was almost certain to lose his own life. Despite this, with outstanding courage and complete disregard for his own safety, he went to the rescue. Willingly accepting the danger, Pilot Officer Mynarski lost his life by a most conspicuous act of heroism, which called for valor of the highest order.* Pilot Officer Andrew Charles Mynarski was only 27 years of age at the time of his tragic death.

In action elsewhere ***Pilot Officer K.O. Moore*** flying a Liberator bomber sank two U-Boats in 22 minutes on June 8. Within days of their June 15th transfer from Britain to France,

Air Force Blue

Canadian Fighter Wing shot down 26 enemy aircraft. Over the Atlantic *#162 Canadian Bomber Reconnaissance Squadron* sank four U-Boats. And, the largest convoy ever assembled, 167 ships, was safely escorted to Britain by the Canadian Navy in mid July.

The *Catalina Flying Boat* is a twin-engine amphibian aircraft developed in 1936 for the U.S. Navy. Its sculptured boat-like hull enables it to make landings and take-offs from water. The Catalina has wheels imbedded in the sides of its hull that can be lowered to convert the Catalina into a land-based aircraft. Bubble canopies midpoint on the sides of the fuselage provide excellent observation of the ground or sea. Twin machineguns were usually mounted in the observation bubbles. The plane is capable of carrying a one-ton load of bombs or depth charges.

The Canadian Air Force favored a version of the Catalina known as the *Canso*. The Canso was preferred for anti submarine patrols because of its ability to remain aloft up to fifteen hours. The flying boat's greatest drawback was its top speed of only 115 miles per hour.

Flight Lieutenant David Hornell was attached to #162 Canadian Bomber Reconnaissance Squadron based in Iceland. On June 24, 1944 Hornell set out on his 60th operational mission. He was the pilot of a Canso flying boat carrying seven other crewmembers: co-pilot, flight engineer, navigator, radio operator, bombardier, and two gunners.

David Hornell was born in Mimico, Ontario January 26th 1910. He attended Toronto's Western Technical School and was working for a rubber company when war broke out. David

Contempt for Danger

enlisted in the Canadian Air Force June 8, 1941. After earning his wings Hornell was stationed at airbases in Prince Edward Island and British Columbia prior to shipping overseas. While in Iceland, Hornell was promoted to Flight Lieutenant, equivalent in rank to a captain in the army.

On the morning of June 24th Hornell's patrol had been airborne several hours and was searching a patch of the Atlantic near the Shetland Islands off the coast of Scotland. Observers spotted a surfaced U-boat traveling at high speed below the Canso's left wing. Knowing that German submarines could submerge in less than a minute, Hornell attacked without hesitation.

The bomber rattled and vibrated as it began a full-throttle power dive. In hopes of engaging the U-boat before it crash-dived the Canso's gunners withheld fire to allow Hornell to maneuver the Canso as close to the submarine as possible before being sighted by the enemy. They got their wish!

As soon as the submarine altered course the Canso's gunners opened fire; scoring hits on the conning tower. The sub's return fire was fierce and accurate. Although it was diving at full power the Canso most likely appeared as a giant lumbering kite to the submariners. The Canso's right guns jammed just as two large holes appeared in the wing. The right engine burst into flame; as did the wing itself. Shrapnel burst through the plane's thin skin of stressed-metal.

Only brute strength and determination enabled Hornell to pull his crippled aircraft out of the power-dive. Here is how the London Gazette of July 28, 1944 reported the situation. *Ignoring*

Air Force Blue

the enemy's fire, Flight Lieutenant Hornell carefully maneuvered for the attack. Oil was pouring from his starboard wing; and the petrol tanks were endangered. Meanwhile, the aircraft was hit again and again by the U-boat's guns. Holed in many places, it was vibrating violently and was very difficult to control.

The London Gazette added: *Nevertheless the captain decided to press home his attack, knowing that with every moment the chances of escape for him and his gallant crew would grow more slender. He brought his aircraft down very low and released his depth charges in a perfect straddle. The bows of the U-boat were lifted out of the water; it sank and the crew were [sic] seen in the sea.*

Hornell's citation also described the Canso's last moments. *Flight Lieutenant Hornell contrived, by superhuman efforts at the controls, to gain a little height. The fire in the starboard wing had grown more intense and the vibration had increased. Then the burning engine fell off. The plight of the aircraft and crew was now desperate. With the utmost coolness the captain took his aircraft into the wind and, despite manifold dangers, brought it safely down on the heavy swell. Badly damaged and blazing furiously, the aircraft rapidly settled.*

The crew was only able to salvage one dinghy before the Canso went down. The raft was too small to hold all eight crewmembers, so they took turns in the water hanging on to the sides. Supplies and safety equipment were lost when the dinghy capsized. The crew was able to right the raft, but two men soon succumbed to exposure. The survivors no longer had anything of use to bail seawater from the dinghy. Hornell subjected himself to greater exposure when he removed his pants and tied the legs together to fashion a bailing scoop.

Contempt for Danger

Search aircraft finally sighted them. A plane dropped a lifeboat 500 yards downwind. *The men struggled vainly to reach it and Flight Lieutenant Hornell, who throughout had encouraged them by his cheerfulness and inspiring leadership, proposed to swim for it, though he was clearly exhausted. He was with difficulty restrained. The survivors were finally rescued after they had been in the water for 21 hours. By this time Flight Lieutenant Hornell was blinded from crusted salt, and completely exhausted. He died shortly after being picked up.*

Hornell's Victoria Cross citation continues: *He well knew the danger and difficulties attending attacks on submarines. By pressing home a skillful and successful attack against fierce opposition, with his aircraft in a precarious position, and by fortifying and encouraging his comrades in the subsequent ordeal, this officer displayed valor and devotion to duty of the highest order.* David Ernest Hornell was thirty-four years of age when he died.

Ian Bazalgette was born in Calgary, Alberta October 19, 1918. When he was five years old his family moved to Toronto, Ontario where Ian attended Balmy Beach Elementary School. When his family moved to England, Ian's education continued at Rokeby School in Wimbleton, and through a private tutor. A month before his 22nd birthday Ian Bazalgette was commissioned as a second lieutenant in the British Army. A year later, in 1941, Ian transferred from the army to the Royal Air Force. In April 1944 he was posted to *#635 Pathfinder Squadron* as a flight commander. Within three months Squadron Leader Bazalgette won the *Distinguished Flying Cross* for action on a mission over Italy.

Air Force Blue

On August 4, 1944 Squadron Leader Ian Bazalgette was designated *master bomber* for a raid on Trossy St. Maximin, France. His Lancaster was to mark the target for the main bomber force. Enemy flak was extremely heavy on the approach to the target and Bazalgette's plane was hit several times. Both starboard engines were knocked out. Serious fires ignited in the fuselage and right wing. His bombardier was wounded. Nevertheless, Bazalgette pressed on with his burning aircraft to mark and bomb the target accurately.

As soon as the bombs were released, the Lancaster went into an almost uncontrollable dive. Expert airmanship and great exertion enabled Bazalgette to regain control. His left inside engine failed and the right wing was now a mass of flames. The mid-upper gunner was overcome with fumes. Squadron Leader Bazalgette ordered those able to do so to bail out.

The London Gazette of August 17, 1945 reported his Victoria Cross citation. *He remained at the controls and attempted the almost hopeless task of landing the crippled and blazing aircraft in a last effort to save the wounded bomb aimer and helpless air gunner. With superb skill, and taking great care to avoid a small French village nearby, he brought the aircraft down safely. Unfortunately it then exploded and this gallant officer and his two comrades perished.* The Gazette added: *His heroic sacrifice marked the climax of a long career of operations against the enemy. He always chose the more dangerous and exacting roles. His courage and devotion to duty were beyond praise.* Squadron Leader Ian Willoughby Bazalgette was 25 years of age when he died in the line of duty.

Contempt for Danger

Lesser known heroes of the skies simply performed their duty, flight after flight. For instance there were the *Night Intruder* teams who risked their lives harassing Luftwaffe fighter bases along the paths of bomber routes. *George Stewart* from Hamilton, Ontario was a Night Intruder pilot. *Paul Beaudet* from Montreal, Quebec was his navigator. George was twenty, Paul a year or two older. Both held the rank of Flying Officer - equivalent to an army first-lieutenant. Their de Havilland Mosquito fighter-bomber was armed with four 20 mm cannons, four .30 caliber machineguns, and two five hundred pound bombs. Canadian factories built more than one thousand of the twin-engine Mosquito aircraft. Constructed mainly of wood and fabric material, the Mosquito's powerful engines enabled it to clock 400 miles per hour and reach altitudes six miles above sea level. Mosquitoes served in a variety of military assignments: escorting Allied bombers, photo reconnaissance, as aerial artillery, and on night intruder missions.

Stewart and Beaudet flew fifty operational missions together. Here is an account of their thirty-ninth night intruder assignment. At their afternoon briefing Stewart and Beaudet learned Bomber Command's target for the night. Their squadron code was *Cricket*; their flight code thirty-four. *Cricket 34* drew Ardorf Airfield as its primary target; Marx and Varol airfields as alternates. Cricket 34 took off shortly after dark. The Mosquito skimmed the North Sea five hundred feet above sea level, keeping below the scope of enemy radar. Flying low also enabled the aviators to spot aircraft silhouettes overhead.

Air Force Blue

Cricket 34 rose to 4,000 feet as it cleared the Dutch coastline. Diving and weaving as it moved inland the Mosquito leveled off at 1,500 feet. Beaudet relied on the glitter from moonlit canals and waterways to help him track a northeast route toward the Zuider Zee. As they approached the vicinity of Ardorf, Stewart and Beaudet were surprised to observe an illuminated runway – the Luftwaffe was landing aircraft.

Quickly dropping down to 500 feet Stewart toggled his master-gun-switch to the *fire* position. Glancing skyward Flying Officer Stewart spotted a German aircraft flying downwind preparatory to coming in for a landing. Stewart opened fire with his cannons, hitting the nose of a German *Junkers 88* night-fighter. The runway abruptly went dark. Stewart glimpsed another 'bogie' silhouetted against the sky circling the field. Moving in fast pursuit Stewart deftly maneuvered his Mosquito closer to the enemy, opening fire just as their flight paths crossed. The enemy, now lower, disappeared into darkness.

Cricket 34 patrolled the area for another ten minutes before turning back to the almost darkened airfield. Red flares warned of a crashed plane on the runway - possibly the Junkers 88. Sweeping over Ardorf Airfield Stewart loosed his bombs. As the Mosquito banked to the left Stewart and Beaudet witnessed two explosive eruptions on the runway. *Cricket 34*'s mission was complete.

36
Battle for Europe

In their drive toward Caen, Canadian troops liberated Carpiquet, France on the 4th of July 1944. Five days later Caen fell to a joint Anglo/Canadian assault. In a non-battle incident members of a German SS Grenadier Regiment *shot and murdered 140 captive Canadian soldiers.*

South of Caen Canadian land forces suffered heavy casualties in an attempt to relieve pressure on American troops about to stage a major breakout. Following the breakout an entire German army was threatened with encirclement by rapidly advancing Allied forces. Unfortunately, the speed of the Allied advance resulted in disaster for both sides; enemy as well as Allied land forces.

On August 8th two flights of U.S. Army Air Force B-17 *Flying Fortresses* bombed-short, causing hundreds of casualties amongst Canadian, Polish and American troops. 3rd Canadian Infantry's commanding officer, Major-General Rod Keller was among the wounded that day. On August 14th a mix-up in signals resulted in Royal Air Force bombers killing 65 Canadian ground troops, wounding another 240. There were also 65 Polish casualties. Four days later RAF Bomber Command again dropped bombs on Canadian and Polish forces, killing 150, wounding 400.

Battle for Europe

Dave Currie was born in Sutherland, Saskatchewan July 8, 1912. David attended Central Collegiate and Moose Jaw Technical School where he learned auto mechanics and welding. He joined the militia in 1939. In January 1940 Dave Currie became a commissioned officer in the regular army. He was promoted to captain in 1941 and to major in 1944.

Major Currie was in command of a small mixed force of Canadian tanks, self-propelled anti-tank guns, and supporting infantry in Normandy. On August 18, 1944 Currie was ordered to cut-off a primary escape route the Germans were using to flee the Falaise pocket. Currie's men encountered stiff resistance near the village of St. Lambert-sur-Dives. Two of his tanks were quickly immobilized when holed by shells from German 88 mm guns.

St. Lambert-sur-Dives was under heavy mortar fire when Major Currie entered the village at dusk alone and on foot. He first reconnoitered German defensive positions, and then proceeded to extricate his crews from their disabled tanks.

At dawn of the following morning Major Currie without benefit of artillery or air support led an attack on the village. German tanks, guns and infantry were well dug-in and opposition was fierce. Yet by noon the Canadian force had secured half the village.

Major Currie skillfully organized the group's defensive positions. For the next 36 hours the Canadians repulsed countless enemy counterattacks. On one occasion Major Currie knocked out a Tiger tank that had been harassing them by personally directing gunfire from his command tank. In another attack while the guns of his command tank fired on other targets, Currie stood erect in the turret using a rifle to pick off enemy snipers. On the one occasion when infantry reinforcements were able to reach Currie's outfit, the major personally saw to their deployment.

Fighting remained heavy. As night fell on August 20th the enemy mounted a major assault to dislodge the Canadians. The Canadian line held. When the German attack diminished, Major Currie swung over to the offensive. Seven enemy tanks, twelve 88 mm guns, and forty vehicles were destroyed. 300 Germans were killed. 2,100 Germans including 500 wounded were captured. More importantly, by overrunning the village, fleeing German armies were denied one of the critical escape routes from the Falais pocket.

The London Gazette reported this about Major Currie's Victoria Cross citation. *Throughout three days and nights of fierce fighting Major Currie's gallant conduct and contempt for danger set a magnificent example to all ranks of the force under his command. There can be no doubt that the success of the attack on and stand against the enemy at St. Lambert-sur-Dives can largely be attributed to this officer's coolness, inspired leadership and skillful use of the limited weapons at his disposal. The courage and devotion to duty shown by Major Currie during a prolonged period of heavy fighting were outstanding and had a far-reaching effect on the successful outcome of the battle.*

After the war David Currie worked eight years for a paper company in Baie Comeau, Quebec latterly as an equipment superintendent. In 1953 he relocated to Montreal to become

Battle for Europe

vice president of a manufacturing company. In 1959 Prime Minister John Diefenbaker appointed David Currie Sergeant-at-Arms in the House of Commons. David Vivian Currie died in Ottawa on June 20, 1986, a month prior to his 74th birthday.

4th Canadian Armored, having freed the town of Falaise, raced to meet up with General Patton's U.S. 3rd Army approaching from the opposite direction. In the ensuing four day battle enemy losses of men and materiel were near catastrophic. The results may well have been even more debilitating for the panicking Germans had the Canadian assault teams been more swift in closing their side of the pincer. American and British commanders were astonished to learn Canadian forces had paused to regroup before attempting to close the gap. The Canadian Army relieved its field commander following an investigation of the incident.

On August 25 Paris was freed by contingents of French and American troops under the command of General Charles de Gaulle.

Seven days later, on September 1st, Canadian troops liberated Dieppe. Following a victory parade through the town the Canadians moved on to free other French channel ports of German occupation troops. The coastal campaign ended with the taking of Calais a month later.

Although British forces had liberated Antwerp, Allied shipping was denied access to the great Belgian seaport because the fifty mile Scheldt Estuary snaking from the Atlantic to the city remained in German hands. General Eisenhower's

201

Contempt for Danger

headquarters considered ship access to Antwerp essential to victory as it was the only port large enough to provide adequate supplies for the four million Allied troops now on the continent. The task of clearing the Scheldt Estuary of over one hundred thousand deeply entrenched Wehrmacht fell to *1st Canadian Army* temporarily under the command of General Guy Simonds.

Both sides of the Estuary, which was actually in the Netherlands, were controlled by the Germans. Canadian troops first liberated the south shore, and then took the enemy by surprise with a waterborne assault of the north bank. However, to reach the Scheldt's westernmost point, Walcheren Island, the Canucks had to negotiate an intricate network of canals, dykes and sodden farm fields. General Simonds ordered a controlled flooding of Walcheren, forcing the Germans to abandon many fortifications in favor of higher ground. A second seaborne landing led to Canadian victory. 1st Canadian Army sustained 6,400 casualties during the bloody five week campaign. Within days the port of Antwerp was opened to Allied shipping.

Guy Granville Simonds, the son of a British Army officer, was born in Edmunds, England in 1903. Young Guy immigrated to Canada at an early age. He graduated from Royal Military College in 1925. As a lieutenant, Simonds served with the Canadian Horse Artillery regiment in Petawawa and Winnipeg. In 1938 Captain Simonds became an instructor at Royal Military College. Promoted the following year Major Simonds transferred to 1st Infantry Division and shipped overseas in 1940. In November 1940 he was recalled to Ottawa

Battle for Europe

and assigned the task of designing a program for the Junior Officer War Staff Course. Guy Simonds did well and within two years became a brigadier general in command of 1st Infantry Brigade. In 1943 he was a major general and led 1st Canadian Division in the invasion of Sicily as well as the Italian mainland. Simonds was in charge of 5th Armored Division when he received his promotion to lieutenant general in January 1944 and given command of 2nd Canadian Corps then training for the invasion of France. In the fall of 1944, during the Battle of the Scheldt, Simonds assumed temporary command of the entire 1st Canadian Army while General Crerar was recovering from serious illness. Simonds was engaged in every major campaign the Canadian Army fought in Europe. Immediately following the war Simonds accepted a posting to the Imperial Defense College in London. His next assignment was commander of Royal Military College in Kingston. Simonds served as Chief of the General Staff from 1951 through 1955. Guy Granville Simonds, a dedicated and much decorated Canadian hero, died in 1974 at the age of 71.

On the Italian front Canadian tanks broke through the Gothic Line south of Rimini in late August following a three week offensive. Near Santa Maria di Scocciano a Canadian unit advanced so rapidly it became separated from the main thrust. A German officer yelled to the cut-off Canadians: "English gentlemen you are surrounded, surrender or die." A Canadian private was cheered when he hollered back: "We ain't English, we ain't gentlemen and, goddamn it, we ain't gonna surrender!" Canadian infantry and armor took the Coriano

Contempt for Danger

Ridge south of Rimini on September 13th. A week later they took the San Fortunato Ridge near the Po Valley where 1st Canadian Corps was obliged to fight a succession of river crossings under intense fire. This was about the time the now famous *Canadian/US Special Forces* unit - the Devil's Brigade - made its successful sea-borne landing on the French Riviera.

37
Smokey Smith

Canadian flying ace *Buzz Beurling* shot down his 30th enemy plane while over France in September 1944. Weeks later Canadian Air Force pilots were the first to shoot down a German jet fighter – Hitler's latest secret weapon. The following day Canadian 6th Bomber Group lost only two planes out of 239 sent on a strike over Dortmond, Germany.

Ernie Smith was born in New Westminster, British Columbia May 3, 1914. Ernie attended Herbert Spencer Elementary School and Trapp Technical High School. Ernie was a construction worker when he enlisted in the Canadian Army. He was known to his buddies as Smokey.

Smokie was with the Seaforth Highlander Regiment, 2nd Brigade, 1st Canadian Infantry Division when it was ordered to establish a bridgehead across the Savio River, Italy on the night of October 21st, 1944. In fact the Seaforths spearheaded the attack.

Torrential rains had caused the Savio to rise six feet in five hours. Owing to soft muddy riverbanks no tanks or artillery could be taken across the raging river to support the rifle companies. Nevertheless the infantry crossed the river under heavy enemy fire and captured their objective. The Germans, however, counterattacked before the Canadians could

205

Contempt for Danger

consolidate their right flank. They hit the tenuous Canadian toehold with three Mark V Panther tanks, two self-propelled guns plus infantry.

Smokey Smith was leader of a three-man PIAT team. The 32-pound hand-held PIAT launches a 2-pound bomb and is considered effective within 300 feet of its target.

With their company under heavy fire Smokey led two men across a road and open field to position their PIAT. Smokey and one of the men returned to their platoon to retrieve a second PIAT. On the way back they encountered an enemy tank lumbering down the road spewing machinegun bullets along the ditches. When his buddy fell wounded, Smokey rose from the ditch and aimed his PIAT. The tank was scarcely 30 feet away when Smokey opened fire, scoring a direct hit. German infantry leaped from the back of their disabled tank firing sub-machineguns and lobbing grenades. Smokey grabbed his Thompson sub-machine gun, rushed to the middle of the road and fired point-blank at the advancing Germans. He killed four outright, six others fled.

Smokey Smith scrambled back to the ditch but hardly had chance to catch his breath before another German tank and more infantry opened fire. Smokey quickly reloaded and, standing astride his wounded buddy, fired at the tank's turret. Smokey's brazen action apparently startled the German commander because the tank stopped, then quickly withdrew leading the German infantry with it. Smokey carried his buddy to a medical aid station then returned to his forward position.

Smokey Smith

The London Gazette reported Ernest Smith's Victoria Cross citation. *By the dogged determination, outstanding devotion to duty and superb gallantry of this private soldier, his comrades were so inspired that the bridgehead was held firm against all enemy attacks pending the arrival of tanks and anti-tank guns some hours later. 1st Canadian Division moved through the bridgehead and went on to capture San Giorgia Di Cesena preparatory to advancing on the Ronco River.*

After the war Ernest Smith worked for a photographic studio in New Westminster, British Columbia; latterly he became a travel agent. Smokey reenlisted in the army during the Korean War. Before retiring from the army in 1964, Sergeant Smith served as a Canadian Forces recruiter in Vancouver; subsequently he was attached to Headquarters of British Columbia Army Command. In November 1995, Smokey Smith then 81, was appointed a member of the Order of Canada. In 2003 Ernest Alvia Smith, Canada's sole surviving Victoria Cross winner, was honored in a ceremony held at Buckingham Palace in London, England. In May 2005 Smokey attended the Netherlands' 60th Anniversary celebrations of the end of the war in Europe. Smokey Smith died three months later. He was 91.

In November, 1944 retired *General Andy McNaughton* was appointed Minister of National Defense. Later that month Ottawa reversed its previously held policy of refusing to send draftees overseas. Until this time conscripts had the option of being assigned to *any military theater*, or remaining in Canada. The vast majority volunteered for any theater and, as such,

Contempt for Danger

were entitled to wear *Canada* shoulder patches on their uniforms as well as a *GS* symbol (denoting General Service) on their lower sleeve. The 60,000 conscripts who refused overseas service were derisively referred to as *Zombies* by the media and public at large. Now the federal government had withdrawn the option of serving only in Canada by ordering 16,000 *Zombies* to Britain. Prime Minister Mackenzie King's government handily won a vote of confidence in Parliament over its amended policy. Also in 1944 the RCMP's patrol vessel *St. Roch* returned to the west coast via the Northwest Passage, this time taking only 86 days.

1st Canadian Army was placed on full alert in mid December when the Wehrmacht unexpectedly launched a powerful attack through the Ardennes Forest that carved a huge bulge in American defenses. By year-end the German thrust had been blunted yet not entirely repelled. On December 29 **Flight Lieutenant Dick Audet** downed five enemy planes in ten minutes.

During the course of 1944 Canada's Navy lost two destroyers, *Athabaskan,* and *Skeena;* frigate *Valleyfield;* corvettes *Regina, Alberni* and *Shawinigan;* and minesweeper *Clayoquot.*

38
Camp X

Few Canadians knew of the existence of *Camp X*, a 175 acre farm on the north shore of Lake Ontario between Whitby and Oshawa. It was established in 1941 by spymaster *William Stephenson*. Camp X was the Allies' first institutionalized spy training camp. Here students learned survival techniques. They were trained in hand-to-hand combat, silent kill skills, the use of firearms and explosives, radio operations, encoding, disguise, and psychological warfare. Graduates were sent to Scotland for commando training, then to England for parachute training. Control over secret agents was overseen by the British SOE – *Special Operations Executive*.

Bill Stephenson was born in Winnipeg, Manitoba January 11, 1896. Stephenson was badly wounded in 1916 while serving as a sergeant with the Canadian Engineers. When he recovered, Stephenson was transferred to the Royal Flying Corps. Pilot Stephenson downed twelve enemy aircraft before being shot down and taken prisoner by the Germans in July, 1918. In the early stages of the Second World War William Stephenson was appointed head of British Security Coordination based in New York City and assigned the code name *Intrepid*. Stephenson earned a U.S. Presidential Medal of Merit for his counter-intelligence work with the Office of Strategic Services,

Contempt for Danger

forerunner of today's U.S. Central Intelligence Agency. His wartime exploits have been featured in several books as well as a major motion picture *A Man Called Intrepid* starring David Niven. William Stephenson died in Bermuda in 1989, age 93.

Camp X was also a key routing station for coded communications between Canada, Britain and the United States. The camp was dismantled following the war.

Canadian secret agent **Guy Bieler** was arrested by *Gestapo agents* – German secret police - in January of 1945. Bieler was a married father of two children when he enlisted in the Canadian Army in Quebec. He was a serving officer with the *Regiment de Maisonneuve* when his unit sailed for England in 1940. Bieler volunteered for service with the *Special Operations Executive* (SOE). In 1942 Bieler parachuted into Occupied France near Paris. Agent Bieler trained 25 armed French Resistance teams to blow-up railroad lines, and derail German supply trains before being apprehended by the Gestapo. Gustave (Guy) Daniel Bieler was tortured by the Gestapo then executed by firing squad.

John Macallister and Frank Pickersgill were both graduates of the University of Toronto. John earned his Bachelor of Arts in 1937, Frank a Master of Arts two years later. Both volunteered to spy for the SOE.

Rather than accept a position as law department lecturer with the University of Toronto **John Kenneth Macallister** enlisted in the Canadian Army. He volunteered for service with the SOE and in 1943 parachuted into Occupied France to conduct sabotage and espionage with the French Resistance.

210

Camp X

John was apprehended in a car waiting to clear a traffic checkpoint and turned over to the Gestapo where, to his surprise, he met up with Frank Pickersgill.

Frank Pickersgill was touring Europe on his bicycle when war broke out. He along with thousands of enemy aliens was arrested and incarcerated in a labor camp. Using a saw blade smuggled to him in a loaf of bread Frank cut through his bars and made good his escape to England. The British recruited him for the SOE. Like Macallister, Pickersgill was dropped into Occupied France in 1943. He was arrested by the Gestapo. Frank almost escaped his captors a second time when he smashed a guard with a bottle and dove through a second floor window. He landed on a Paris street where he was shot and dragged back into the building. John Macallister and Frank Pickersgill were transferred to Buchenwald Concentration Camp, tortured and executed. Only three out of the ten Canadians dropped into Occupied France prior to D-Day returned alive.

Aurora, Ontario resident *Joseph J. Gelleny*, a Camp X graduate, was captured in Hungary in 1944. The Canadian army lieutenant was one of the few secret agents to survive torture by the Gestapo. The Gestapo liked to condition prisoners being held for questioning by depriving them of sleep. Day or night, and always without warning, prisoners were dragged from their cells into a brightly illuminated room where they were beaten mercilessly with fists, truncheons and steel rods. Slow extraction of toe nails and finger nails helped encourage prisoners to divulge secrets. Another Gestapo

Contempt for Danger

favorite involved sequentially breaking the knuckles, wrists and elbows of prisoners, then leaving their wounds untreated.

On several occasions the soles of Joe Gelleney's feet were beaten raw with rubber hoses while he was strapped to a gurney. Electrodes were attached to Gelleney's toes; then a hand generator was cranked, sending electric jolts of fiery pain up his legs; the faster it was cranked the more excruciating the pain. The Canadian's worst screams emanated when the electrodes were attached to his genitals. Joe Gelleny escaped during the disorganization preceding the collapse of the Hungarian regime. He was taken into custody by advancing American forces who, after confirming his identity, turned him over to the British.

First Lieutenant Joseph J. Gelleny was discharged from the Canadian Army in 1945. Finding all Ontario universities full, Joe obtained funding under the Canadian Veterans Loan Act to attend university in Fort Wayne, Indiana. After attaining his Bachelor of Science degree Joe Gelleny pursued his Masters at the University of Toronto. Joe married his high school sweetheart Helen Mossey and established a successful business in Toronto. Helen and Joe were blessed with three children and ten grandchildren. Helen died in 1999. Joe continues to split his retirement between Aurora, Ontario and Clermont, Florida.

39
Penetrating the Reich

More than a 1,000 Canadian artillery guns opened fire in February 1945 launching an Allied campaign to clear German forces from west of the River Rhine. Harry Crerar, a full general since October 1944 was in command.

Henry (Harry) Duncan Graham Crerar was born in Hamilton, Ontario in 1888. Harry graduated from Royal Military College in Kingston in 1909 and was serving with the militia when World War I broke out. As an artillery officer Harry fought in Flanders as well as on the French front. By war's end Harry was a lieutenant colonel serving with Canadian Corps general staff. Crerar completed studies at the Imperial Defense College in London during the 1930s. Back in Canada Crerar served a stint as Director of Military Operations and Intelligence at National Defense headquarters in Ottawa before assuming command of Royal Military College. In 1939 Brigadier General Crerar was called back to Ottawa. A year later he was appointed Chief of the General Staff. In 1941 Crerar shipped overseas to assume command of First Canadian Corps. Three years later, in March 1944, Harry Crerar replaced Andy McNaughton as commanding general of First Canadian Army. At the pinnacle of his career in 1945 Harry Crerar commanded 450,000 troops - 13 divisions including 4 Canadian, 9 British, plus units of Americans, Belgians, Dutch

213

Contempt for Danger

and Poles - the largest military force ever commanded by a Canadian.

Following his retirement from the army in 1946 Harry Crerar joined the diplomatic corps and held postings in Czechoslovakia, the Netherlands and Japan. Harry Crerar died in Ottawa in 1965 at age 77, having devoted a lifetime of service to his country.

Aubrey Cosens was born in Latchford, Ontario May 21, 1921. He grew up in Porquis Junction near Iroquois Falls, Ontario. At 17 Aubrey quit school to take a job on the railroad working alongside his father. He tried to join the Air Force at the outbreak of war but his application was rejected.

The following year Aubrey joined the army. Between 1940 and1943 he was promoted twice, and saw service in Canada, Jamaica and Britain. In 1944 Cosens was promoted to sergeant.

On the night of February 25, 1945 *1st Battalion of the Queen's Own Rifles Regiment* attacked the hamlet of Mooshof, Germany. Taking Mooshof was considered critical to the development of future operations.

Two tanks were supporting Sergeant Cosens' platoon when they attacked three farm structures. German resistance was stiff. Twice the Canadian assault was repelled. The officer in command was killed when a fierce enemy counterattack almost annihilated the platoon.

Cosens assumed command and directed the four survivors to provide covering fire. Under mortar and machinegun fire Cosens raced across open ground to the one remaining tank.

Penetrating the Reich

He was exposed as he stood in front of the turret directing the tank's fire. The German counterattack faded.

When a second counterattack was successfully repulsed, Sergeant Cosens ordered the tank to attack the farm buildings. Cosens and his four infantrymen followed closely. After the tank rammed the first building Cosens entered alone. He killed several defenders outright, and took the remainder prisoner.

Ignoring intense machinegun and rifle fire, Sergeant Cosens entered the second and third buildings alone, personally killing or capturing all the occupants.

Immediately following this extraordinary feat, Sergeant Aubrey Cosens was shot through the head by an enemy sniper. He died instantly.

In commenting on Sergeant Cosens' Victoria Cross citation the London Gazette reported: *The outstanding gallantry, initiative and determined leadership of this brave Non Commissioned Officer who himself killed at least twenty of the enemy and took an equal number of prisoners, resulted in the capture of a position which was vital to the success of the future operations of the Brigade.* Sergeant Aubrey Cosens was twenty-three years of age when killed in action the morning of February 26, 1945. He is buried in Groesbeek Canadian War Cemetery, Nijmegan, Holland.

Freddie Tilston was born in Toronto, Ontario June 11, 1906. He attended De La Salle High School, the Ontario College of Pharmacy and the University of Toronto. Fred was sales manager for a drug manufacturing company when in 1940, at age 34, he enlisted in the army as a private.

215

Contempt for Danger

Tilston adapted well to army life. Age and education contributed to his early promotion to sergeant, and subsequent commission as a second lieutenant. By 1945 he was a major.

At 0715 hours on March 1st, 1945 *2nd Canadian Division* launched an attack through the *Hochwald Forest*, the last fortified German defense line west of the River Rhine. Tanks could not be used because of mushy ground. The *Canadian Essex Scottish Regiment* was tasked with taking Udem then clearing the northern half of the forest. Major Fred Tilston was a company commander with the Essex Scottish.

Major Tilston faltered only momentarily when he suffered a head wound while leading his company across five hundred yards of open country under intense enemy fire. With his sub-machinegun blazing, Tilston directed his men through a ten-foot entanglement of barbed wire before reaching the enemy trenches. He charged a machinegun post, lobbing a hand grenade to put it out of action.

Leaving one of his platoons to mop up, Tilston led an attack against the enemy's second line of defense. As he approached the edge of the woods a bullet wound to the hip knocked him to the ground. He continued to shout instructions to his men while struggling to his feet. It required vicious hand-to-hand fighting to dislodge the Germans from their network of trenches and dugouts. Despite his wounds Tilston continued to inspire his men as they systematically cleared the earthworks of a stubborn enemy. They had overrun two German company headquarters. However, the toll had been great. Tilston's company had suffered 75% casualties.

Penetrating the Reich

Mortar and machinegun fire preceded a German counterattack. Major Tilston crept from platoon to platoon, organizing their defense against the advancing enemy. German troops came within hand-grenade range but were unable to penetrate Tilston's defense line.

When ammunition ran short Tilston made his way under heavy fire to another Canadian company. In fact he made several trips to bring bullets and grenades to his beleaguered troops. He also brought back a radio to re-establish contact with battalion headquarters.

On his third dash Tilston was wounded a third time. The major was discovered in a shell crater beside a road bleeding from wounds to his head, hip and leg. Although barely conscious, he declined medical attention until he had reviewed their defense plan with his one remaining officer.

The London Gazette reported this about Major Tilston's Victoria Cross citation: *By his calm courage, gallant conduct and total disregard for his own safety, he fired his men with grim determination and their firm stand enabled the regiment to accomplish its object of furnishing the brigade with a solid base through which to launch further successful attacks to clear the forest thus enabling the division to accomplish its task.*

The gravity of Major Tilston's wounds necessitated the amputation of both legs. Yet scarcely a year later indomitable Fred Tilston returned to his former employer in Canada where he was appointed vice president of sales. He was subsequently promoted to president, eventually becoming chairman of the board. In 1963 Fred Tilston was appointed Honorary Colonel of

Contempt for Danger

his former regiment. Frederick Albert Tilston died in Toronto, Ontario September 23rd, 1992. He was 86.

1st Canadian Corps, comprising *1st Infantry and 5th Armored Divisions*, had slogged its way almost to the top of Italy when orders were received directing it to link-up with *1st Canadian Army* in northern Europe. The 93,000 Canadians who served on the Italian front had suffered over 26,000 casualties. Almost 6,000 Canadian servicemen remain buried in seventeen cemeteries across Italy. The U.S. Navy transported Canada's soldiers around the Italian boot to the French seaport of Marseilles. *1st and 5th divisions* then rolled overland through France and Holland to link up with Canada's 2nd, 3rd, and 4th divisions. General McNaughton's dream of uniting all Canadian land forces in Europe had finally come true.

40
Victory In Europe

Canadian airborne troops and air force squadrons added their weight to the Allied push east of the Rhine on March 24, 1945. The airborne dropped from twin-engine Douglas Dakota aircraft. Overhead Canadian fighter aircraft provided a protective shield for Canadian troops parachuting onto German soil.

Freddie Topham was born in Toronto, Ontario August 10, 1917. Sometime following his attendance at Runnymede Collegiate Institute Fred Topham hired on with a mining company in Kirkland Lake. With the outbreak of war he joined the army and became a medical orderly with 1st Canadian Parachute Battalion.

1st Canadian Para dropped on the strongly defended area of Wesel, Germany. Close to midnight Corporal Topham was treating casualties when a call came in for the rescue of a wounded soldier lying in an open area. Corporal Topham witnessed two medical orderlies gunned down in quick succession as they hovered over the wounded man.

With grim determination Corporal Topham dashed forward through enemy fire. Topham made it to the casualty and was working on the wounded man when he was shot through the nose. Despite severe bleeding and acute facial pain

Contempt for Danger

Topham never faltered. He quickly administered first aid to the wounded soldier and, although under fire, carried the man to the wooded shelter of the Canadian lines.

Refusing medical help for his own wound, twenty-seven year old Topham continued to rescue other wounded men lying on the battlefield. Enemy fire was heavy and accurate. Two hours later, when all casualties had been cleared, Fred Topham consented to having his own wound cared for. The Medical Officer wanted to evacuate Topham from the forward perimeter to the safety of the Canadian main line, but Topham declined, insisting he be allowed to return to his outfit.

The day was sunny and mild as Corporal Topham made his way toward his company. Suddenly the enemy launched a mortar attack. Topham came across an officer warning everyone to keep clear of a blazing Bren Gun carrier whose ammunition was exploding. Corporal Topham could see Canadian soldiers trapped inside.

Without regard for his own safety, Topham raced to the carrier and extracted its three occupants. He brought all three men back individually across open territory under enemy fire. One of the rescued Canadians died shortly afterward. The other two were safely evacuated from the perimeter.

The London Gazette said this of Corporal Frederick George Topham's Victoria Cross citation: *This Non Commissioned Officer showed sustained gallantry of the highest order. For six hours, most of the time in great pain, he performed a series of acts of outstanding bravery, and his magnificent and selfless courage inspired all those who witnessed it.* Upon his return home to East York, Ontario a

Victory In Europe

grateful community named a street and a neighborhood park in honor of their hero. Fred Topham, a lineman for a local power company, was just 57 years of age when he died in Toronto March 31, 1974.

In early April, *1st Canadian Army* liberated Zutphen, Holland; a week later Apeldoorn. Fighting along the Canadian front came to an abrupt halt when the German commander of the Netherlands agreed on a temporary truce to permit Allied aircraft to drop food to starving Dutch families.

U.S. President Franklin Delano Roosevelt died April 12, at age 63. Vice President Harry S. Truman was sworn in as Roosevelt's successor. Two weeks later Italian partisans machinegunned Benito Mussolini and his mistress, Clara Petacci, then hung them upside down in a Milan plaza. Two days later Adolf Hitler, Fuhrer of the Third Reich, committed suicide in Berlin.

The Canadian Navy reported the loss of corvette *Trentonian* February 22, minesweeper *Guysborough* on March 17, and minesweeper *Esquimalt* on April 16. The *Esquimalt* was torpedoed by a German U-boat outside Halifax harbor. Thirty-nine of Esquimalt's crew perished.

Canadian *6th Bomber Group* conducted its final bombing mission of World War II on April 25th. Earlier in the month Canadian Navy cruiser *Uganda* was transferred to the U.S. Fifth Fleet in the Pacific to assist in the shelling of Okinawa and the Japanese mainland.

On the home front Montreal Canadiens' hockey star *Maurice 'Rocket' Richard* achieved an unprecedented National Hockey League record by scoring 50 goals in fifty games.

Contempt for Danger

The public finally learned that Japan had bombed farms in British Columbia and the prairies. The bombs fell after riding high above the Pacific Ocean suspended beneath thirty foot-wide paper balloons. The bomb laden balloons drifted all the way to North America from Japan. In the absence of serious damage or injuries the federal government had requested the media to withhold reporting the incidents in order to deny Japan the results of their bombing missions. In May of 1945 the government lifted its publishing ban.

A day following the Canadian Army's capture of Oldenburg, Germany on May 4th the front fell eerily quiet in anticipation of the Reich's unconditional surrender to the Allies. It happened in a schoolhouse on May 7th when American, British and Soviet generals signed an agreement with a German delegation to officially end hostilities the next day. *VE Day - Victory in Europe* - came on May 8, 1945. The Soviet Union commemorates the end of the Patriotic War, as World War II is known there, one day later on May 9th.

The Canadian Government immediately rescinded the law allowing the army to send non-volunteers overseas. Henceforth only those who voluntarily signed-up for General Service would be eligible for overseas duty. Apart from 40,000 Canadian troops earmarked to participate in the Allied Army of Occupation the Government was anxious to bring home its troops in Europe.

Repatriation was based on the number of points earned. Points were awarded for length of time in service, time overseas, and time in combat zones. Married personnel scored

Victory In Europe

higher than single status. Additional points were earned by volunteering to fight in the Pacific Theater. At its height 3,000 men and women a day were released from Canada's Armed Forces. Returning personnel were granted 30 days leave and given cash bonuses based on points earned. Government funds for schooling and graduate programs were readily available.

41
Victory Over Japan

Almost fifty nations including Canada met in New York City to endorse the World Security Charter creating the United Nations. Prime Minister William L. Mackenzie King's Liberal Party easily won the June federal election. Not all national leaders were so fortunate, however. Across the sea Winston Churchill was defeated in Britain's general election. Churchill was succeeded as prime minister by Clement Atlee. In July Canadian troops took up positions in Berlin to share in the occupation of the former German capital.

Prime Minister King insisted that only volunteers would serve with Canadian Forces in the war with the Empire of Japan; estimated to be another two years of bloody fighting. In July volunteers began to mass at Canada's nine assembly centers.

Eighty thousand Canadians volunteered to fight in the Pacific, about twenty-five percent greater than the Government need. The Department of Defense planned to send two Army divisions to the Pacific after completing advance training with the U.S. Army in Kentucky. The Air Force would send fifteen thousand personnel along with their squadrons of bombers and transport aircraft. The Navy committed to 14,000 men and sixty ships.

224

Victory Over Japan

As it turned out *Uganda* was only Canadian Navy ship to serve in the Pacific Theater. And it too was withdrawn in late July. In keeping with Canada's *volunteers only* policy the cruiser was ordered to return home in July after scarcely one third of its crew opted to continue fighting. Uganda had seen active service in the Atlantic prior to shifting to the Pacific in April. Not able to relate to Canada's volunteers only policy American and British seamen were miffed by what appeared to be desertion by an ally. Uganda received a cool reception when it stopped over in Pearl Harbor for refueling.

Several significant events occurred in August 1945. 100,000 Japanese died at Hiroshima after a single *atomic bomb* was dropped from a U.S. Army Air Force B-29 on August 6th. Two days later the USSR declared war on Japan. The Soviet Union had been the only fighting nation to battle Germany yet remain at peace with Japan. On the 9th a second *atomic bomb* killed 40,000 at Nagasaki, Japan.

Bobbie Gray was born in Trail, British Columbia November 2, 1917. He grew up in Nelson. After completing high school Bob Gray spent a year at the University of Alberta in Edmonton before moving to Vancouver to complete his education at the University of British Columbia.

In 1940 Bob Gray was one of seventy-five candidates selected for a naval commission. Hammy, as he was now known, and twelve other cadets subsequently qualified as pilots in the Fleet Air Arm. Following training as a fighter-bomber pilot Sub-Lieutenant Gray was assigned to the Royal Navy's aircraft carrier *HMS Formidable*.

Contempt for Danger

Not long after being promoted to full naval lieutenant (equivalent in rank to an army captain), Gray was cited in 1944 for *'brilliant work during an attack on the German battleship 'Tirpitz' in Alten Fjord, Norway'*. In late 1944 HMS Formidable shifted from the Atlantic to the Pacific Theater. In July Lieutenant Gray earned a *Distinguished Service Cross* for assisting in the destruction of a Japanese destroyer near Tokyo.

On August 9th, 1945 Lieutenant Gray flew his Avenger fighter-bomber from the flight deck of HMS Formidable for the last time. Gray was leading an attack on Japanese shipping in the vicinity of Honshu Island when the fliers discovered several Japanese ships at Onagawa Bay. Gray's flight of Avengers immediately attacked.

Japanese army batteries on the ground joined warships in the bay in sending up a furious rate of fire at the diving aircraft. Lieutenant Gray selected a destroyer as his personal target. Oblivious to the concentrated fire, Gray made straight for his target. His Avenger was hit again and again. As he drew closer to the destroyer his plane caught fire. Fifty feet from the Japanese ship Gray released his bombs; scoring at least one direct hit, possibly more. The enemy destroyer sank almost immediately. Lieutenant Hampton Gray did not return.

The November 13th 1945 issue of the London Gazette reported Lieutenant Gray's Victoria Cross citation. *Gray was leader of the attack, which he pressed home in the face of fire from shore batteries and at least eight warships. With his aircraft in flames he nevertheless obtained at least one direct hit which sank its objective.* Robert Hampton Gray, age 27, died August 9, 1945 in

Victory Over Japan

the service of his country; the 41,371st and last Canadian to die in battle during World War II.

VJ Day – Victory over Japan – came on August 14, 1945. The formal surrender signing took place aboard the battleship USS Missouri in Tokyo Harbor on September 2nd.

For Canada the Second World War lasted six long years; from September 1939 to September 1945. One in ten Canadians - over one million men and 43,000 women - served in Canada's armed forces during World War II; all but 60,000 of whom volunteered to serve as overseas combatants. Canada's military sustained 96,500 casualties.

With 730,000 men and women clad in khaki the army was easily Canada's largest military force. 22,500 soldiers died in action.

At its peak Canada's Air Force had 215,000 personnel and 78 operational squadrons. 60,000 of the 100,000 Canadian airmen stationed in the European theater were attached to the Royal Air Force; approximately 25% of the RAF's strength. 17,000 Canadian airmen died in battle, 10,000 while serving with Bomber Command. 131,500 air crew graduated from the Commonwealth Air Training Program during its 5-1/2 years of existence.

Of the ninety-five thousand men and women who donned Canada's naval uniform 1,900 lost their lives escorting over 25,000 ships to Britain. From humble beginnings of just thirteen ships in 1939, Canada's 378 fighting ships comprised the world's third largest fleet at sea by war's end.

Contempt for Danger

Number and Classification of
Canadian World War II Fighting Ships

2 cruisers

2 escort carriers manned on behalf of the Royal Navy

3 armed merchant cruisers

28 destroyers, six lost

70 frigates, one lost

123 corvettes, ten lost

80 minesweepers, four lost

16 armed yachts, two lost

16 motor torpedo boats comprising 2 flotillas.

Approximately 12,000 merchant marines sailed with Canada's civilian navy. They crewed freighters and tankers laden with food and war supplies. Slow convoys of merchant ships plowed the Atlantic at less than 10 knots per hour. Faster convoys moved at a pace of 10 to 15 knots. The very fastest ships invariably traveled independently. 73 Canadian merchant ships were sunk during the war.

Newfoundland sent almost twenty thousand troops overseas. Over one thousand were wounded in action. Seven hundred never came home.

Canadian military uniforms were scarcely distinguishable from their British counterparts. Apart from *'Canada'* shoulder patches both countries wore similar uniforms and earned the same classification of medals. The highest award for bravery in battle was the Victoria Cross. Sixteen Canadians were awarded the Victoria Cross for heroism during the Second World War.

Victory Over Japan

World War II
Victoria Cross Honor Roll

Squadron Leader **Ian W. Bazalgette**	**Air Force**	on a mission over N.E. Europe 1944
Sergeant Aubrey Cosens	**Army**	at Mooshof, Germany 1945
Major David V. Currie	**Army**	at Falais Gap, France 1944
Captain the Reverend **John W. Foote**	**Army**	at Dieppe, France 1942
Lieutenant **Robert H. Gray**	**Navy**	mission over Onagawa Bay, Japan 1945
Major Charles F. Hoey	**Army**	at Maungdaw, Burma 1944
Flight Lieutenant **David E. Hornell**	**Air Force**	over the North Atlantic 1944
Major John K. Mahony	**Army**	at Melfa River, Italy 1944
Lieutenant Colonel **Charles C. Merritt**	**Army**	at Dieppe, France 1942
Pilot Officer **Andrew C. Mynarski**	**Air Force**	on a mission over Cambrai, France 1944
Sergeant Major **John R. Osborn**	**Army**	at Hong Kong 1941
Captain Frederick T. Peters	**Navy**	at Oran, Algeria 1942
Private Ernest A. Smith	**Army**	at Savio River, Italy 1944
Major **Frederick A. Tilston**	**Army**	at Hochwald Forest, Germany 1945

Contempt for Danger

Corporal
Frederick G. Topham   **Army**   near the Rhine River, Germany 1945

Captain Paul Triquet   **Army**   at Casa Berardi, Italy 1943

Epilogue

Following cessation of hostilities panels of international jurists sat at Nuremberg, Germany and Tokyo, Japan presiding over trials of military and civilian officials accused of crimes against humanity during World War II.

Canada paid the United States $108 million for the 1,200-mile Canadian stretch of the *Alcan (Alaska-Canada) Highway* built as a military artery during the war. In the spring thousands of tulips burst into bloom in Ottawa, a gift of eternal friendship to the people of Canada from a grateful Netherlands. And every May since then the Ottawa Tulip Festival has attracted thousands of visitors to Canada's capital.

Princess Juliana, later Queen of the Netherlands, and her husband Prince Bernhard moved to the safety of Ottawa in 1940 and remained there for the duration of the war. On January 19, 1943 the princess gave birth to her third daughter, Margriet at Ottawa Civic Hospital. Canadians are also fondly remembered by Dutch citizens for liberating much of their nation in 1945.

The war effort cost Canadian taxpayers over $20 billion. In addition, Canadians invested hundreds of millions in Victory Bonds and War Savings Stamps. Private and community *Victory Gardens* provided fresh produce and stimulated citizen morale. Scarves, socks, and gloves were knitted for troops overseas. Blood donors from across the country received honorable mention, pins and badges.

Meat, sugar, tea, coffee, and butter were rationed. Only 12 ounces of alcohol could be purchased a week – in some provinces the limit was as little as 12 ounces per month. Owners of private cars had to make do with three gallons of gasoline per week. There were no new appliances, cars, tires or inner tubes. The national slogan was: *Use it up. Wear it out. Make it do.*

Blackouts were common in coastal regions. Inland, the country settled for brownouts - no neon signs or non essential illumination. While travel passes were not required, the public was discouraged from making unnecessary trips by bus or rail – coining the phrase *'Is this trip necessary?'*

The federal *Wartime Prices and Trade Board* established production quotas and approved consumer prices. Neighborhoods and schools rallied to the cause by collecting old newspapers and scrap metal. Other street collection drives were organized to salvage rubber, surplus kitchen fat, bones and rags.

A million women entered the work force - full and part time - accepting most any job that freed men for military service. The majority were employed in munitions and other war production factories. Hundreds of thousands worked on farms. Over forty thousand women enlisted in the armed forces. Another 650 women served overseas with the Canadian Red Cross Corps.

The Canadian Red Cross, founded in 1900, began preparations for a wartime role in 1939. The *Canadian Red Cross*

Epilogue

Corps was formed and by 1945 had sent 641 volunteers overseas. Red Cross women served in Britain, France, Italy and North Africa performing vital roles such as ambulance drivers, nurses, relief workers and administrative assistants. After the war the Red Cross facilitated in the transition of thousands of wounded veterans to civilian life.

Fewer than 40,000 students were enrolled in Canadian universities prior to the war. By the late '40s the student population had doubled. This dramatic increase was almost entirely attributable to the enrolment of 35,000 war veterans. *By comparison at the end of the 20th Century more than 600,000 students were enrolled in Canadian universities.*

45,000 Canadian Armed Forces personnel got married while serving in foreign duty stations. Their spouses, or *war brides*, came mostly from the British Isles.

For 126 years Canada relied on the *military-honors-systems* of her allies to recognize conspicuous heroism of Canadian Forces during battle. In 1993 the Government of Canada introduced the *Victoria Cross Canadian Version* bearing the Latin inscription *PRO VALORE*. The award is open to members of Canadian Forces as well as allied armed forces serving with Canadian battle groups. As of 2005 there have been no recipients of the *Victoria Cross Canadian Version*.

Index of Heroes

ALGIE, Wallace Lloyd, 117
AUDET, Richard 208

BARKER, William George, 81
BARRON, Colin Fraser, 71
BAZALGETTE, Ian W., 194
BEAUDET, Paul, 196
BEURLING, George 'Buzz', 205
BELLEW, Edward Donald, 40
BENT, Philip Eric, 65
BIELER, Guy, 210
BISHOP, William Avery, 80
BOOMER, K. A., 150
BOURKE, Roland Richard Louis, 87
BRERETON, Alexander Picton, 93
BRILLANT, Jean, 92
BROWN, Harry, 57

CAIRNS, Hugh, 118
CAMPBELL, Frederick William, 42
CLARKE, Leo, 48
CLARK-KENNEDY, Wm. H., 96
COCKBURN, Hampden Zane C., 29
COMBE, Robert Grierson, 56
COPPINS, Frederick George, 93

235

Contempt for Danger

COSENS, Aubrey, 214
CRERAR, Harry, 213
CRUICKSHANK, Robert E., 87
CROAK, John Bernard, 90
CURRIE, Arthur, 57
CURRIE, David Vivian, 199

De WIND, Edmund, 86
DINESEN, Thomas, 93
DOUGLAS, Campbell Mellis, 4
DUNN, Alexander Roberts, 1

FISHER, Frederick, 40
FLOWERDEW, Gordon Muriel, 102
FOOTE, John Weir, 155

GILLENY, Joseph J., 211
GILDAY, Tom, 178
GOOD, Herman James, 91
GRAY, Robert Hampton, 225
GREGG, Milton Fowler, 113

HALL, Frederick William, 41
HALL, William Edward, 3
HANNA, Robert Hill, 60
HARVEY, Frederick M. W., 100
HEWITT, D. A., 138
HOBSON, Frederick, 58

Index of Heros

HOEY, Charles Ferguson, 172
HOLLAND, Edward J. G., 29
HOLMES, Thomas William, 66
HONEY, Samuel Lewis, 110
HORNELL, David Ernest, 191
HUTCHESON, Bellenden, 107

KAEBLE, Joseph, 91
KELLER, Rod, 183
KERR, George Fraser, 111
KERR, John Chipman, 49
KINROSS, Cecil John, 68
KNIGHT, Arthur George, 105
KONOWAL, Filip, 60

LAWSON, J. K., 145
LEARMONTH, Okill Massey, 59
LYALL, Graham Thomson, 112

MACALLISTER, John K. 210
MacDOWELL, Thain Wendell, 54
MacGREGOR, John, 115
MAHONEY, John Keefer, 174
McCRAE, John, 39
McKEAN, George Burdon, 86
McKENZIE, Hugh, 69
McLEOD, Alan Arnett, 77
McNAUGHTON, Andrew, 169

Contempt for Danger

MERRIFIELD, William, 116
MERRIT, Charles Cecil I., 153
METCALF, William Henry, 106
MILES, G. R., 140
MILNE, William Johnstone, 54
MINER, Harry G. B., 92
MITCHELL, Coulson Norman, 116
MOORE, K. O., 190
MULLEN, George Harry, 68
MURRAY, Leonard W., 144
MYNARSKI, Andrew Charles, 189

NICKERSON, William Henry S., 27
NUNNEY, Claude Joseph P., 104

O'HEA, Timothy, 6
O'KELLY, Christopher P. J., 67
O'LEARY, Michael, 36
O'ROURKE, Michael James, 60
OSBORN, John Robert, 146
OTTER, William, 21

PATTISON, John George, 55
PEARKES, George Randolph, 70
PECK, Cyrus Wesley, 105
PETERS, Frederick Thornton, 161
PICKERSGILL, Frank, 211

Index of Heros

RAYFIELD, Walter Leigh, 108
READE, Herbert Taylor, 3
RICHARDSON, Arthur H. L., 27
RICHARDSON, James Cleland, 49
RICKETTS, Thomas, 117
ROBERTS, J. Hamilton, 157
ROBERTSON, James Peter, 70
RUTHERFORD, Charles Smith, 95

SCRIMGER, Francis A. C., 41
SHANKLAND, Robert, 67
SIFTON, Ellis Welwood, 54
SIMONDS, Guy, 202
SINTON, John Alexander, 44
SMITH, Ernest 'Smokey', 205
SPALL, Robert, 95
STEELE,SamuelBenfield, 24
STEPHENSON, William, 209
STEWART, George, 196
STRACHAN, Harcus, 101

TAIT, James Edward, 89
THOMPSON, Richard Rowland, 20
TILSTON, Frederick Albert, 215
TOPHAM, Frederick George, 219
TRIQUET, Paul, 167
TURNER, Richard Ernest W., 29

Contempt for Danger

WESTLAKE, Albert 187
WESTLAKE, George 187
WESTLAKE, Thomas 187
WILKINSON, Thomas Orde L., 45

YOUNG, John Francis, 108

ZENGEL, Raphael Louis, 94

Bibliography

A Nation Forged in Fire by J.L. Granatstein & Desmond Morton. Lester & Orpen Dennys, 1989.

A Short History of Canada by Desmond Morton. McClelland & Stewart, 2000.

Canada: A People's History Vol 2 by Don Gilmour. McClelland & Stewart, 2001.

Canada: A Political and Social History by Edgar McInnis. Holt, Rinehart & Winston, 1982.

Chronicle of Canada conceived by Jacques Legrand. Chronicle Publications, 1990.

Chronicle of the World conceived by Jacques Legrand. Chronicle Communications Ltd, 1989.

History of the Canadian Peoples: 1867 to the Present by Alvin Finkel, Margaret Conrad, and Veronica Strong-Boag. Copp Clark Pitman, 1993.

The Illustrated History of Canada edited by Craig Brown. Key Porter Books, 2000.

Juno by Ted Barris. Thomas Allen Publishers, 2004.

The London Gazette, select issues 1940 through 1946.

Maclean's Canada's Century by Maclean-Hunter Publishing. Key Porter Books, 1999.

Marching As To War by Pierre Berton. Doubleday Canada, 2001.

A Military History of Canada by Desmond Morton. Hurtig Publishing, 1990.

Testaments of Honour by Blake Heathcote. Doubleday Canada, 2002.

The Tools of War 1939/45 by Reader's Digest Association (Canada) Ltd., 1969

Veteran Affairs Canada websites.